C000100077

Testimonials

"I could not put this book down. And as soon as I finished reading it, I read it again. And maybe one more time after that … *The Whimsical Rebel: Break People-Pleasing Addiction without Becoming an Asshole* is a must-read for anyone needing to learn how to better love and understand themselves. Ahdri Kent offers unparalleled, intuitive, and endearing insights into why we people pleasers do what we do.

With her raw language, captivating stories, and profound guidance, Kent gives readers someone to relate to and lovingly accepts exactly who they are. It's okay to want to please others; that makes us special. But we need to learn how not to lose ourselves in the process. This book made me laugh, cry, gasp, and sigh … It was an emotional ride in the best of ways. Along the way, I gained valuable knowledge that has changed my entire outlook on my life and relationships. Experiencing so many "AH-HA!" moments in this book, I have come to better understand myself and others. Kent has given me the tools I desperately needed but never knew I was missing."

– Nancy Graham-Tillman

"This book was a hit upside the head I didn't know I needed. I've been asleep to the concepts that the author illustrates with a refreshing sense of authenticity and casual conversational humor. She takes a very serious issue and presents it as if we were friends chatting over coffee. It made this very palatable. Interesting read!"

– Kate M

"I freaking love this book! As a success and leadership coach, I see so many people sidelined by their people-pleasing and perfectionist issues. This no-nonsense, outspoken approach is just what so many people need to take the first step towards their own empowerment. I found myself cheering and shouting as if I were at a church revival. If you're stuck in the world of putting everyone above yourself and then hating yourself for it afterward, and you like a direct non-apologetically aggressive (in all the right ways) approach, this book is for you!"

– Heather Vickery

"This book was so helpful both to help me to identify which type of people pleaser I am (I'm a Mouse!) and to have some concrete steps for shifting out of the people pleasing mindset and into one that is healthier for both myself and those around me."

– Megan Caper

Discover what type of
People Pleasing Addict
you are with this free quiz!

Go to
www.ahdri.com/freequiz

The Whimsical Rebel

The Whimsical Rebel

Break People Pleasing Addiction
without Becoming an Asshole

Ahdri Kent

PUBLISH
YOUR
PURPOSE
PRESS

Copyright © 2021 Ahdri Kent. All rights reserved.

No part of this publication shall be reproduced, transmitted, or sold in whole or in part in any form without prior written consent of the author, except as provided by the United States of America copyright law. Any unauthorized usage of the text without express written permission of the publisher is a violation of the author's copyright and is illegal and punishable by law. All trademarks and registered trademarks appearing in this guide are the property of their respective owners.

For permission requests, write to the publisher, addressed "Attention: Permissions Coordinator," at the address below.

Publish Your Purpose Press
141 Weston Street, #155
Hartford, CT, 06141

The opinions expressed by the Author are not necessarily those held by Publish Your Purpose Press.

Ordering Information: Quantity sales and special discounts are available on quantity purchases by corporations, associations, and others. For details, contact the publisher at orders@publishyourpurposepress.com.

Edited by: Nancy Graham-Tillman
Cover designed by: Jayne Goodall
Typeset by: Medlar Publishing Solutions Pvt Ltd., India

Printed in the United States of America.
ISBN: 978-1-955985-03-1   (hardcover)
ISBN: 978-1-951591-97-7   (paperback)
ISBN: 978-1-951591-98-4   (ebook)

Library of Congress Control Number: 2021914342

First edition, September 2021

The information contained within this book is strictly for informational purposes. The material may include information, products, or services by third parties. As such, the Author and Publisher do not assume responsibility or liability for any third-party material or opinions. The publisher is not responsible for websites (or their content) that are not owned by the publisher. Readers are advised to do their own due diligence when it comes to making decisions.

The mission of Publish Your Purpose Press is to discover and publish authors who are striving to make a difference in the world. We give underrepresented voices power and a stage to share their stories, speak their truth, and impact their communities. Do you have a book idea you would like us to consider publishing? Please visit PublishYourPurposePress. com for more information.

Disclaimer:
The stories of my life are recollected from my perspective with the utmost intention to represent them as clearly and faithfully as possible. Some names have been changed.

The stories of my clients have been altered in ways only to protect their requested anonymity.

I assume no liability for loss, damages, or hurt feelings caused by these retellings and/or omissions.

I do not claim to be a healthcare professional. This book does not replace the advice of a medical or mental healthcare professional. Consult your doctor or therapist before making any changes to your regular physical or mental health plan.

Dedication

For Katrina

You loved me before my eyes were open

You loved me when you felt unseen

You loved me when I couldn't see myself

You love me still by healing with me now

The following words are for the tiny us's.

The littles running barefoot on the farm.

Contents

INTRO-
DUCTION

A: Be a People Pleasing addict.
B: Be an assertive asshole.

Um ... I'll take hidden option C:
Live and act from a place of LOVE,
abundance, trust, authenticity, and
alignment. Thanks for playing though!

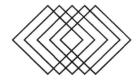

The Unbuyable Birthday Present

I pick up the phone and feverishly type out the following words: "Turns out I won't be able to make it tomorrow. <Insert list of valid but redundant reasons here>. But I still want to get a gift to you! What do you want for your birthday?"

Long pause and then … "All I wanted for my birthday was for you to be here."

After that response, I wouldn't hear from my best friend of over 13 years for nearly three months.

At first, I was filled with indignant shock that I shared with everyone who would listen.

"After everything I've done for her? Every party I HAVE made it to? All the last-minute travel plans I've pulled out of my ass? Thirteen years of being there for her and ONE party is somehow the last straw?"

Then came the projections.

"What, just because I don't have kids, I'm held to a higher standard of putting my life on hold for everyone else?"

The onslaught of tit-for-tats.

"I've lived over two hours away for eight years now, and I can count on one hand the times she has come to visit me versus the multiple times a year I moved mountains to visit her."

More projections.

"So I'm being punished for not staying in our hometown?"

The list of audacious questions continued to grow as further proof of my innocence. But there's one thing my Pleasing Addiction wouldn't allow me to do.

ACKNOWLEDGE WHAT WAS ACTUALLY UPSETTING ME.

I hid behind the devastation of "letting someone down" and scurried down the rabbit hole of why I didn't deserve to feel bad. I had a list of things I had done for her, all so I wouldn't feel like a complete shit-heel now that I had disappointed her. But the list didn't do its job. I still had DONE the actual disappointing, and reciting the list wasn't going to free me from my anxiety.

Why? Because none of it mattered. I had created the list as a scapegoat for the inevitable, but it did absolutely nothing to protect me.

Failure to Communicate

I wouldn't discover for years what I was truly upset about. It had nothing to do with Sean and everything to do with the anger I felt in myself for over-extending my heart, body, and energy as some sort of fucked-up protection against future liability.

Have you ever said to yourself, "It's OK if I sit this one out, I've been to all the others" or "It's OK if I'm late, because I'm normally on time"?

Those are the first telltale signs that your lists of deeds for others is complete bullshit.

Do you know why it's OK that you sit this one out? BECAUSE YOU'RE ALLOWED TO RESPECT YOUR ENERGY!

Do you know why it's OK that you're late? BECAUSE IT'S A FACT AND IT'S NOT GOING TO CHANGE BY FREAKING OUT ABOUT IT!

Nobody is ever "ok" because you previously paid some energetic price to buy your innocence. They will only be "ok" if you communicate your needs with truth and transparency. The reality is, all your past gifts and deeds can't possibly predict your loved one's needs now.

But I still don't know this yet, and that lack of acknowledgement impeded me as a communicative, compassionate person. It also made the next step impossible.

ASKING SEAN WHAT WAS ACTUALLY UPSETTING HER.

Because, c'mon. She was a 28-year-old woman. My cancelation to her birthday party wasn't the REAL issue.

Is it our job to hash out what "someone's problem" is? No. But is it our responsibility to usher in clear communication with full transparency of our own emotions in the relationships we hold dear? You are GODDAMN RIGHT IT IS. And, despite feeling emotionally battered in the moment, our relationship was dear to me.

The communication ban was lifted with a text war at 4 a.m. one morning. We never really worked through it, but it felt resolved enough to move forward. We just had a new acceptance that our friendship would never really be the same because clearly ... it was never what either of us thought it was to begin with. And I wouldn't learn what was actually going on and recognize my patterns of addiction until years later. That fight was almost exactly eight years ago.

Could a friendship avoiding near destruction be the big takeaway of this story? Sure, if that makes you feel good in your britches. But the real takeaway for me will always be the introduction to my list of bullshit.

Now let's take a look at yours.

The Signs of People Pleasing Addiction

It's not always about the list, but if you have one, it's definitely a sign you're a People Pleaser. Here are a few more if you're not quite sure:

- Have you ever found yourself blindsided at having disappointed someone?
- Do you ever catalog the ways in which you've helped someone to validate why they shouldn't be disappointed?
- Do you find yourself seeking praise in other relationships to deafen the conflict you're feeling in another?
- Do you find yourself responding to "I love you" with a cute "Love you more!"?
- Do you say "whatever is easiest for you" even in situations where it doesn't really apply (insert awkward stare from barista)?
- Do you find yourself having conversations in your head before actually speaking with someone?
- Do you have trouble staying and feeling present even in the good times?

If you've picked up this book, you've either already had that "are you fucking kidding me?!" moment or you can just feel the pivot creeping up behind you. Either way, you know you can't unsee the shit that needs changing. You are ready. That change is NOW.

Being Overextended and Underappreciated

Before we get into helping YOU, let's talk a little bit more about ME, not just because I love me some me but because you need to know why you should even listen to me!

For one thing, I have the history, the dark dangerous romance with this behavioral addiction. For decades (prior to the pivotal moment above) I sold my soul for the approval, acceptance, and affection of others.

And it didn't just start with me (it's a little early on in the book to get all eye-rolly, so we will talk about the impact our parents have on us a bit later). My family was THE family that always showed up. Whenever anyone in the community had any kind of emergency or tragedy or need, we would be there ... with casseroles, cleaning supplies, money, and the determination to fix anything. Everyone knew they could call on us, and like a Kent woman Bat-Signal, we'd be there. "Selfless service" was how we approached the world.

Then, after my 16th birthday ... catastrophe hit.

My dad died.

Auto-erotic asphyxiation. Those words made about as much sense to a 16-year-old daddy's girl as "accidental suicide." In a singular moment, he and his entire identity were gone. And the sudden shattering of it all was a trauma I didn't know how to process, so I would internalize it and the warped lessons it continued to teach me. The unsaid message, "If you trust your desire … you will die," was seared deep into the tissue of my heart.

It would be another 16 years before I would break that subconscious belief and absorb the true message that who we TRY to be isn't what we leave behind. In the wake of destruction, all that's left is the pain and the wondering, "If only they had made their mental health, intimacy, sex, and ego a priority …"

In the meantime, almost overnight, all my family's repressed bullshit and dysfunction came roaring up to the surface and FAST.

Years of emotional neglect, lack of self-care, and REALNESS came up. The trauma was intense. It was a crazy 180-degree shift from an idyllic, fairytale childhood to realizing our family dynamic was actually incredibly toxic.

So I did the only thing I knew how to do at the time: I leaned in even HARDER to forcing love on others, and caregiving.

I immediately went out and found someone to take care of.

I got married. At 16.

I then spent the next seven years working jobs I had no interest in, enrolling in culinary school to support my husband, and generally playing out a variety of self-sacrificing martyr programs.

That's right! I went to college for a degree I had NO interest in to support someone else. Looking at it now, I know it sounds insane ... but when you're inside the bubble of People Pleasing Addiction, it seems like the only option.

So whether you see these patterns in yourself right now, or you're still not sure if this is for you, really focus on how this makes you FEEL.

Do you have a sinking feeling in your gut?

Do you hear your inner captive self saying, "MmmHmmmmmmm!"?

Is your FEAR already trying to sabotage your emotional growth by whispering in your ear, "But who will love us if we change?"

Or maybe you feel something is just OFF in your world, but it's hard to put a finger on it, because you're doing everything "right" but you're still so tired ... and so unhappy.

Whatever you're feeling right now ... it's OKAY!

The hardest step is acknowledging, admitting even, that you want change.

It's hard, but worth it! Because life becomes a million times more magical and exciting once you break free from this addiction! So cuddle up with these pages and allow yourself to take the stage for once. You'll be surprised how the spotlight can change every perception you've ever had about this incredible life that is indeed YOURS.

Perception Cubes

"You need to calm down this instant!" my dad declared in a deep, stern, Castilian voice.

"I CAN'T!" I yelled back.

"Why?"

"'Cause Trina's bein' a BITCH!"

My dad tried not to laugh as he grabbed my arm and pressed me down into the chair at the breakfast table. He slapped a notebook and a pen down in front of me. I rolled my eyes and released a ridiculous audible sigh that never got me out of shit before, but I refused to remove it from my eight-year-old tantrum repertoire.

"Do it," he demanded as he pointed to the pad and pen.

"This is so stupid," I mouthed as I relented and began doodling a 3D cube.

"Why do we do this?" he asked in a soft, but take-no-shit tone.

"To calm down or whatever," I muttered as I drew the last line and moved onto the next cube.

"Stop it. Why do we do this?"

I always appreciated his patented second chances. They gave me the freedom to be bratty for a bit before willingly participating in the life lessons I knew were gold but didn't want to admit.

"I don't know…" I'd lie just so I could hear him tell me again.

He scooted closer and pointed to one of my poorly doodled cubes. "Which square is on top?"

"This one!" I'd point to the not-so-obvious square every time.

He would smile and slowly raise his eyebrows before delivering the punch line …

"But what if it's not?" we'd say in unison.

I would stick my tongue out and squint my eyes, shifting my vision to make the cube change direction on the paper.

While behind me, he would softly continue the lesson: "It doesn't make your sister wrong just because she doesn't agree with you. And it doesn't make you wrong for not changing your mind. But it makes you absolutely wrong to tell someone they're wrong for not sharing your perspective."

He would pat my head almost too hard with his massive bear paw and tell me to go apologize to my sister for acting like a dictator, which I never would. But the lesson stuck, and I think that's all he really wanted.

Today a version of my father's Perception Cube is tattooed on my right wrist and is ever so appropriately the logo for my business.

When we allow things to truly impact us, they become lessons we can't unlearn.

P.S.

Sorry for acting like a tiny dictator, Trina.

The People Pleaser's Autonomous Master Program

Once I committed to finding help, I attacked it like I do everything in life—like a woman possessed. But the road was tough. The biggest work I had to do was psychological, around my unconscious program. At first it felt like the most selfish thing in the world. I had to go against EVERYTHING I had been told about myself and what I SHOULD do.

Throwing away years of ideology and conditioning doesn't happen overnight, and I couldn't find ANY

"I leaned even harder into forcing love on others"

resources to help. I found advice for narcissistic abuse victims, but I wasn't in a narcissistic relationship. I found information for men, but well … last time I checked, I identify 100 percent as a ciswoman. I even found resources for anxiety and perfectionism, but I'm 1,000 percent okay with looking like an idiot.

The information I found also didn't tackle the behavioral addiction element of People Pleasing; rather, it just told me to stop doing it. That's like telling someone who is unhappily overweight due to poor self-care to stop eating like an asshole. It doesn't address their addiction to food and comfort.

So I started with the people around me. I looked at my mother and my sister, at these people killing themselves only to be heartbroken, overworked, and underappreciated. I knew I was very different from my mother, and thus began compiling different identities of People Pleasers (which we will further discuss in chapter one).

I then expanded those identities and the unique relationship each one held in my recovery methodology to develop a course, tested it, ran it one-on-one, expanded it to groups, and ultimately developed The People Pleasers Autonomous Master Program—the first course ever released to tackle and conquer this behavioral addiction.

It's the result of years of soul-crafted individualized recovery development, studying, testing methods, going through my own therapy, attending events, and interviewing experts. You name it and I've probably been through it to absorb what would help YOU and I best!

So ... what exactly is in this powerful methodology? It will radically shift your priorities and beliefs and free you from your preconceived notions of self.

In the following chapters you will:

- Determine if you are the Mouse, Phoenix, or Pitbull and why it matters.
- Uncover the true face of your "inner saboteur" and learn the healing powers of saddling up beside it to heal together.
- Learn how to avoid self-induced spirals of shame and abandonment.
- Learn how to stop coaching, lecturing, and teaching so you can start having REAL conversations.
- Develop the mystical manifesting power of a "Nightmare List."
- Learn how to reprogram anxiety to be your ally rather than your enemy.
- Learn how to harness the gift of your empathy rather than relenting to its curse.
- Learn how to develop stronger relationships through conflict.
- Learn how to strengthen your relationship with yourself and begin to rebuild a connection to your true core essence.

- And so many other addiction-shattering, whimsical self loving tools of badassery!

Are you ready to get started? It's time to stop pleasing others and learn to please your-damn-self.

CHAPTER ONE

LONELY
AT THE TOP

*Control, or the illusion of it ...
that's the real C-word.*

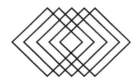

LET ME START by telling you that this process isn't as simple as your deciding that you're no longer going to be abused or taken advantage of. I wish it was that simple but it's not. (But you know that, don't you?)

We're going to be taking a deep look at the toxic patterns that cause your People Pleasing cycles, how to break those patterns, and how to finally be free …

Free to control who you allow into your life.

Free to control what you want to do with your life.

Free to find the love that YOU give so freely to everyone else.

And the first icky pattern we get to look at is the Pleaser's faux value system. It's gonna be super easy to scoff and say, "Ummm, no. I don't think I'm better than other people." But to achieve the breakthrough you so deeply desired when opening this book, you're gonna have to swallow that scoff and hear me out!

You didn't MEAN to. But this addiction builds a ladder, one fucked-up rung at a time, and you propped your fine ass all the way up at the top of it!

You don't even have to agree with what I'm saying. It's a fact. If it weren't, you would be incapable of thinking you were better equipped to handle a situation than the person you're trying to help. You wouldn't think that you know how to word something perfectly so your significant other agrees with you. And you would never utter the words, "If you want something done right, you have to do it yourself."

So whether you're able to truly swallow this value system pattern or whether you just want to chew on it some more ... we can at least agree on this one thing before moving forward: it's fucking lonely at the top! And being at the top brings a lot of fear with it. Let's start by addressing some of these fears.

FEAR 1:
The world will COLLAPSE if you aren't the one holding it together

I promise you, the world will NOT collapse if you don't hold it together. You may have trouble hearing this. You may have an immense fear that if you don't do <fill in the blank>, nobody will. But this fear is tied to your need for control.

Here's the thing. You'll NEVER know what the world is capable of if you never stop doing it all yourself.

By stopping your People Pleasing tendencies, you'll force others to show up for themselves AND you. You'll see your loved ones step up. You'll see your children step up. You'll realize you don't have to do it all.

FEAR 2:
Recovery means changing who you are and how you feel love

You won't change who you thought you were, rather you will DISCOVER who you truly are. You WERE born to love hard. Giving isn't wrong, and you'll learn to hold your boundaries without an induced, inauthentic aggression. You'll learn to respect yourself without having to evoke a nasty, negative, exhausting energy.

You'll uncover your true identity by reading this book—not the identity you had layered on you like a used winter coat by your past lovers, caregivers, society, and guilt.

FEAR 3:
There is no one out there who can love you as hard as you love them

You were born to love hard and that's okay. Giving isn't wrong, and you don't have to start shutting off parts of yourself. Instead you'll learn to live fully in that gift by really feeling and intuitively knowing what people need without it being a vice or a weakness.

You'll learn that loving someone harder IS NOT okay. Your self-worth will start to influence the people you allow into your life. You'll be attractive to the big love from your family, friends, and romantic partners.

You are worthy of all you give to others. Over-loving at the expense of your own energy is a reflection of your feelings of unworthiness.

FEAR 4:
If you recover from this addiction and abandon your post as caregiver, you will disappoint and eventually lose the ones you love

Earning respect doesn't have to cost you self-respect. You ARE supported, you may just not believe it yet. People have grown accustomed to you giving everything that you have, but you don't have to put your self-respect on the line. It's completely possible to recover from a behavioral addiction without losing those who truly love you.

You Can't Save Others

Even more than the fears above, a People Pleaser really fears their loved ones being hurt. This is devastating. We want to save everyone we care about from any sort of emotional conflict or devastation, so we control and control and control everyone and everything around us. Eventually this control manifests in the feeling that if you want something done right you just have to do it yourself.

For some people, that underlying fear goes very deep. Let's talk about my mom for a minute.

Years ago, my sister and I were both adults, and for completely different but equally cringey circumstances, still living under my mother's roof. She requested we get our shit together and move out because of the emotional strain we were placing on her. We gladly obliged and moved out together into a place only ten minutes away.

I quickly realized that I couldn't live with my sister. I wanted to stab her in the eye with a spoon. But I didn't want to hate her, so I told her she needed to move into her own place if we were ever going to speak again. She agreed. Sure, we went through some grieving and some heartache, but we understood that we were saving our relationship and began the exciting journey of finding her and her daughter their own place.

We told my mother, and she lost her shit. She threatened to disown me. She thought I was shoving her daughter and grandchild out into the cold. The situation triggered her like nothing else. When we dug deeper, we realized she actually had a fear of my sister and niece dying. When she lost her ability to control the situation, she feared the absolute worst.

It was about control. But here's the thing. You can't control much in this world, and you can't save anyone. For a Pleaser, the act of "saving" is actually cleverly disguised manipulation. The moment we can accept that is the moment we can find peace in knowing we can only hope to encourage others to save themselves.

The only thing you can control is you.

And the only person you can save is you.

You ARE Worthy of Love

I want to start off by thanking you. Thank you for everything you've done. Thank you for all the times you put everyone else first. Thank you for all the times you were exhausted and still came to someone's rescue.

THANK YOU.

I see all the effort you've put in. I see YOU.

I see the real you, and I'm here to help everyone around you see it. No matter what harsh truths you might face in this book, no matter how much my words may feel like a punch in the gut, I'm on your side.

I lived this. I felt it. Any gross feelings you will have, I had them too. None of what I'm revealing here comes from a place of judgment; rather, it comes from a place of reverence for your strength. You are strong. It took a lot to get here, and it will take a lot to get through recovery. But you can do it. I have faith in you! And if you don't share that faith, please please please borrow mine.

There's a contrast and conflict in living on the cusp of diving into recovery. You're unable to see clearly that you're the catalyst for this hurt, because you really want to find out why you keep letting other people be the catalyst, why you keep attracting toxic people, and why you keep letting neglect happen TO you.

You can't see it clearly, yet you're willing to accept all this responsibility for letting everyone down if you change their perception of you. Those two realities can't exist at the same time. You're in denial about one or the other.

You have to dive in and accept that you set the precedent, and you've continued to own it out of guilt. You've resisted change because of a fear you will let everyone down, and they are used to you doing everything for them.

You dug your own grave. You made your own bed. You have to hold onto that reality, that responsibility, and accept it. And then you'll see how my People Pleasing Addiction (PPA) methodology will teach you a sustainable recovery from People Pleasing Addiction without losing those who truly love you.

The love you give EXISTS FOR you too! Your self-worth dictates reciprocity; YOU are worthy of all you give to others. Over-loving at the expense of your own energy is born from feeling unworthy of potent love yourself.

It bears repeating: Earning respect doesn't have to cost you self-respect. As you go through this book, you may not yet feel supported, but you are. You ARE supported ... it's a fact.

And you will find the love you deserve, and not just from yourself. I promise.

The Proposal, The Bear, and Santa Claus

Here's my story of reciprocated love.

I'm a December baby and a People Pleasing Addict, which means I always have been, and always will be, a Christmas FREAK. My friends, family, clients, and followers are no strangers to this grown-ass woman declaring Santa Claus is REAL from November 1st well into January.

And don't forget, I'm also The Whimsical Rebel. On the surface this means I've dedicated my life to the passion of eliminating People Pleasing Addiction WITHOUT raising the level of toxic dominance in the world.

Low-key it means I LOVE Disney.

So, I'll go ahead and put two and two together for you ... the REAL Santa Claus is the one at Disney World. You're welcome.

2018 was the year my boyfriend at the time, Derren, and I celebrated our 10th Magical Christmas Season together and our fourth season spent celebrating with the REAL Santa in Disney World.

We had planned super-special gifts for one another and had talked and teased about them for weeks. Sadly, neither would come to pass by December 25th. In fact, although mine was late to launch, it at least happened. Derren's gift for me was shot down, kicked in the dick, dragged through the dirt, and died on the battlefield of love.

But more about that later ... back to ME and my astounding gift-giving talents. For the purpose of this awesomeness you should know that Bear was my pet name for Derren. So, my gift for my Bear was a pop-up exclusive-secret-location fancy dinner catered by ... a BEAR. You read that right. Not a real one of course, just a talented man in a bear-chef mascot-style costume. But for the sake of whimsy, you couldn't have told a single person at that table that it wasn't a walking, breathing, exquisite foodie, living bear. And with that kind of whimsy, that kind of Christmas magic, where grown-ups willingly suspend belief as a gift for no one but their inner child ... the romance was bubbling. As were the wine and liquor!

By the time we were delivered home, we were lit and having an absolute ball. We drank some more, talked of Christmas and whimsy and those last ten years together. Then he finally spilled the beans.

"So ... you know my Christmas surprise for you? The one I told you got shot down and I had to abandon the whole plan?"

"Mm'yeahhh?"

"I had done all this preparation. I went to Disney. I stood in line to talk to Santa. I had this printed out picture of you so they'd know who to look out for. And I had the ring to give him ..."

Boom. My heart dropped into my stomach—as the whimsical one's heart does upon hearing the words "Santa" and "the ring" in the same sentence. I tried to hold back the stunned look on my face and let him finish. I failed miserably, because his eyes got wide and he started apologizing ...

"I tried so hard! I told the elf my whole plan to bring you back on your birthday, and when Santa saw us he'd know to surprise you with the ring himself, and that's where it was gonna happen!"

"ERMAHGOFD!" I shouted from beneath my hand forcibly holding my trap shut. My continued disconcerting reaction apparently did not come off as the jubilation I felt but instead came off as anger and disappointment for having been burdened with the information, knowing a Disney World Santa Clause proposal was not how that story ended.

So his voice raised another half an octave to combat what he thought was the flame about to escape my throat and hurriedly continued recounting the demise of the world's best proposal-planning attempt.

"The elf was so excited and told me to go in to ask the manager how to best go about, you know, pulling it off! I was so excited! The elf totally got it! So I did what he said, I walked up into that town square concierge room, found the manager, and revealed my awesome plan, hoping she would be just as excited! She was NOT. She was like a stone gargoyle plucked from Beast's castle." His face fell as he felt her words all over again. "'Absolutely not. I'm sorry, Santa Claus, as well as any other cast members, cannot take part in proposals. If you'd like to propose to her in front of Santa Claus, we can't stop you. But he can in no way be part of the process.'"

"I didn't want to tell you, 'cause I didn't want you to be let down. But it's been ten years! And I couldn't just let you think I didn't even plan anything! I've been waiting for the most perfect way to ask. And it finally came to me, and I got shot down. That's why I was so sad when we talked that day ... and that's why I didn't want to tell you what the surprise that got ruined was. And maybe it's 'cause I'm drunk, but tonight was so special, and I felt like you deserved to know ... how mad are you right now?"

Still suffocated by my own palm, I stared wide-eyed. Giving nothing.

My response came out in a series of chirps, snorts, coughs, and bawling tones. I loved that he loved me that much to try to put something together, even if it failed.

It wasn't the relief of, "Oh thank God, he didn't think ten years together was just like whatever, and actually tried to do something for it!" And it wasn't the thought of being engaged that set off the most unflattering combination of crying and smiling I'm sure he'd ever seen.

Nor was it the painfully obvious, but not yet acknowledged, mile high wall between us that kept a proposal from being either executed OR realistically and mutually taken off the table after a decade spent together.

In that moment, it was simply the crushing reality that someone exists in this world who could love as ridiculously, unprotectedly, and adventurously as I do. Another human existed who could show love, create experiences, and give gifts just as selflessly, wildly, and wholeheartedly as I do.

That's it. That's all. The simplicity of another human being ridiculous with me.

In that moment, a massive thread of People Pleaser, the one guarding my heart, was proven wrong and forced into recovery with the rest of me.

Your People Pleaser Type

Now you know it's possible. Maybe you don't want Disney, Santa, and whimsy, but now you know … no matter the perceived ridiculousness of your capacity to love … like-energy EXISTS out there to reciprocate! Unfortunately, it does take some work. That work starts with the foundation of which TYPE of Pleaser you are.

When I created the program, I landed on three different types of Pleasers: Pitbull, Mouse, and Phoenix. These are all on a spectrum, and there are attributes of each that overlap. And during their recovery, a Pleaser can actually shift from one to the other as their awareness unfolds.

Note: as I interviewed people and put together the quiz, I determined this addiction can absolutely be environmental. I've had clients that didn't have a lick of PPA until they fell into a narcissistic relationship. For others it was handed down as part of their family culture. The key

> is to note that it can appear at any time, to anyone, just like any other addiction. It can take a traumatic event to bring it out, or you may have been raised that way. There are entire families, cultures, communities, and groups of people that are People Pleasers.

There's not one type that is worse than the other, or one that has a more difficult path to recovery; however, the Phoenix is the extreme side of the spectrum, and, if not introduced to recovery, can begin relying on narcissistic behaviors as a survival mechanism. This makes recovery harder to introduce, but never impossible.

To determine your type, just hop over to http://www.ahdri.com and take the free quiz. Within six questions, you'll know which type you best identify with! I strongly suggest discovering your type before diving into the overview I give below.

The Pitbull

If you're the Pitbull, you will fight for anyone. You will bite for anyone. Your fierce loyalty is grounded in love. You have strong opinions and Edward Scissorhands people out of your life who have done you or your loved ones wrong. You have someone, even when they ain't got themselves. But let's not get it twisted now, someone can't throw the ends of the earth you've traveled to in your face the first time you aren't available. Or maybe they can.

Maybe you're the dummy for misplacing your loyalty and love in them. You can't pretend nothing happened, BUT ... if they argue their case eloquently enough, maybe you can be swayed to continue killing yourself for them and their approval.

IN RELATIONSHIPS

Your loved ones, friends, family, lovers ... you know they aren't your competition, right? To you "love you ... love you more" ... those are fightin' words! Going above and beyond is almost a sport for you. You honestly feel you win dedication, loyalty, adoration, and commitment. Meanwhile here you sit, wondering why no one can ever give as much to you ... just once. Spoiler alert, they can't. Because even this version of YOU isn't REAL. It isn't SUS-TAINABLE. It isn't FAIR. But it's no coincidence that Pit-bull is your archetype. Because despite being larger than life in your affections and loyalty ... you'll stay. You'll give up on happiness elsewhere, you'll even die inside. But you'll never stop begging for that one person's affection you had set your sights on. This alone should be proof enough that you honestly DON'T know what's good for you and need a solution.

I'm definitely the type to say, "Shoot for the moon, you'll land among the stars," but this cannot be applied when you're trying to control the moon. What I mean by this is, you have to recognize the control freak in you that is setting an expectation OF disappointment. Because if you KNOW you're going to be disappointed, then you're not surprised. Removing surprise is taking control. This is what you're doing when you demand perfection. You're setting up those around you for failure so that you'll never be surprised. Instead of always proving yourself right, what if you spent your energy proving yourself WRONG? You've stolen the ability from someone to love you perfectly, by deciding that they can't possibly love you as hard as YOU love THEM. Meanwhile ... setting someone up for failure is the opposite of LOVE. So really, who disappointed who?

AT WORK

You're everyone's friend. You're the best at your position. You really DO try your best to be perfect, on time (despite always being late), or take all the extra shifts. So much so that you take personal offense to write ups or ridicule. You need to be the best because you want to prove your loyalty. All archetypes need to be the Teacher's Pet, but yours is secretly rooted in wanting to be their best friend. Keep in mind, you don't need THEM to be YOUR best friend ... you just want to be theirs.

IN HEALTH

You're likely to do whatever your booest of boos is doing. Because you've got their BACK. If they need a cheat day, you wouldn't want them feeling fat ALONE ...

so what's a little ice cream? So what if you haven't had a drink in six months, it's your Boo's bachelorette! = hung the fuck over. You'll often stay overweight so as to not be "unsupportive" of those closest to you. If you're a lucky Pitbull surrounded by fit fanatics, you'll embrace it fully and go Rabdo on their asses to prove it.

The Mouse

If you're the Mouse, you are a "YES MAN." Not because you don't have ideas or opinions of your own, but because personal preference doesn't hold a candle to someone's happiness and the ease with which your relationship is carried out. You are often late, but you'll always come through because you said you would. But you're starting to see how people don't truly appreciate your sacrifices. You don't need recognition, but you think it's gone beyond that now. You might just be worth more than you've been giving to others ... or maybe not ... maybe you're just on your period.

IN RELATIONSHIPS

Your mindset and withholding reality create a quiet, brooding conflict in your relationships. Romantic and otherwise. You take it upon yourself to provide all the love, be it deserved or not, because at some point they showed you love. Once that love was shown, that's all you needed to take up the reins and make everything

OK ... for everyone ... forever. You've resolved many an argument by apologizing and declaring that you're an idiot. And you mean it. You rely heavily on what you mistake for introspection but is really just you avoiding conflict by accepting the blame.

Here's the problem. You are TAKING the opportunity for growth and organic affection right out of the hands of those you think you're protecting from conflict. You're robbing them of the opportunity to figure out their own shit. You're also robbing them of the opportunity to fully realize WHY they should love you. Without this opportunity for realization on their end ... you will never receive the love you deserve, and they'll never get the experience of deciding it's worth giving that love to you. The people you love deserve the chance to develop those feelings and express them in their own way. You're not taking care of anyone, Mouse. You're stealing away their human experience and eventually their chance at reciprocated joy and happiness. You're so desperate to be surrounded by love that you are trying to control it, but your end result is you ... alone ... surrounded by zombies that you created.

AT WORK

The "I'm not worthy" undertow will take Mice down the fastest in their careers/financial situations. Mice have an insanely hard time sticking up for themselves. This doesn't have to be in the face of conflict, it can even be in positive circumstances too. A Mouse might respond to their superior who asks, "How much would you like for your quarterly raise?" with a quiet, "Wow, I mean whatever you think is good …" followed by a nervous laugh. A Mouse will stay in the same job, at the same pay, because they appreciate being given employment and will take the rest on the chin. Entrepreneurship for Mice is especially difficult because entrepreneurs must live in the mindset of abundance, worth, and "Go for No." Hearing "NO" doesn't fuel a Mouse's fire. It extinguishes it. So the internal struggle to stay in the serving mindset of an entrepreneur is almost unbearable.

IN HEALTH

Personal health is hard for ANY type of People Pleaser; however, Mice may find themselves in a pattern of starvation. They are afraid to speak up in social situations for fear of offending someone. If you're underweight*, it's because, secretly, you're not WORTH making sure you're fed. If you're overweight*, it's because you can't tell someone no. (*unhappily so)

The Phoenix

"I'm sorry, but I can't." If you're a Phoenix, you don't even let someone finish excitedly spouting the invitation. Because you're drowning. You've got TOO much to do, to take care of, and none of it makes you HAPPY. You think it does. But it's sucking the life out of you. You have to say NO to the things that may possibly bring you peace and joy, because the world will BURN if you don't fulfill all you've willingly (even sometimes forcefully) put on your plate. But you're starting to feel it. The fire is dying. It's you. You're terrified that you won't be able to warm all of those you've taken under your wings if your fire burns out. But there's something new there … You're so scared of the new feeling you view it almost like a suicidal thought … "What if I quit lighting myself on fire, let them learn to create their own warmth, and allow myself to rise from the ashes?" But is it a suicidal thought if it's only a version of yourself you kill?

IN RELATIONSHIPS

Your relationships (family, romantic, or otherwise) are afflicted. You're such a tornado of get shit done that you've wrapped the way people should feel about you into that cyclone of, "If you want it done right, do it yourself." … But Phoenix, you can't love yourself FOR someone else. You all but kill yourself to PROVE to everyone around you why you deserve their love and respect, but that's not how affections are manifested or developed. No one has ever fallen in love because someone showed them how compatible they are on an expertly written document. Someone who LOVES YOU is not going to love you because you bent over backwards. Believe it or not … that's not why they fell in love with you to begin with.

You've almost scared everyone into being around you. Because who are they to argue with what you DO and all that you SACRIFICE for them? But that's not the same feeling as joy. You're a bully, Phoenix. You've essentially created a loyal following of people who know their role and revere you as the great mother hen you are. You long so badly to control the love you're not sure you can get otherwise that you steal their power to deny you.

AT WORK

You train … everyone. You do … everything. You support the team, your boss, your fellow employees, and even your boss's superiors. That's not to say you don't have enemies, but you would never let some dumb bitch make YOUR office look bad, so you cover her shit too. Your poor significant other/family are on high alert when you come home, because you don't just bring work home with you … you take the office and install it brick by brick in your living room. Eventually you and your loved ones are living in your high-anxiety work zone. Everything = exasperation, frustration, deep sighs, and FMLs. You find solace in people allowing you to vent, because painting the picture for them is the only way you can keep convincing yourself that you deserve the torture and weight you willingly place upon your shoulders ... that the office would burn to the ground were you not there to save it, and that you'll never be appreciated for your daily sacrifice. Entrepreneurship rarely enters the radar for a Phoenix; they're usually too busy getting their third or fourth degree to advance in their current field of work.

IN HEALTH

Ever the fiery mother hen, you're not only gonna prove you can provide meals for your family, you're gonna supply meals for a fuckin army. You're also gonna insist everyone else help you finish those leftovers. If you're underweight, it's because you don't have TIME to meal prep for yourself because your family/job/obligations come first. If you're overweight, it's because you don't have TIME to meal prep because your family/job/obligations come first ... you see the pattern, yes?

The Path of Continued Recovery

Now that you know what type of People Pleaser you are ... I want to stress the importance of getting individualized recovery help for your type. This book contains high-level content for all three types, but in my one-on-one work I create personal plans and super individualized care for your super special type.

Personalized coaching or not, you will feel like a brand-damn-new person by the end of this book!

But for some, implementation is easier read than done, so finding your version of sustainable recovery is going to be key.

No one should ever refer to themselves as a recovered People Pleaser. You should refer to yourself as a "People Pleaser in recovery," because anything can happen. No one can live in 100-percent alignment all the time.

If you fall off the wagon, there is nothing wrong with you. You may find yourself in a narcissistic relationship. A friend may break your trust. Don't burden yourself with guilt and self-loathing; rather, realize these neural patterns are carved in pretty deep, and simply take time—once redirected—to fill back in the space so there now exists neutral ground where there was once a trigger.

You don't have to start all over from the beginning. You own the wagon now, so if you fall off it, you don't need to catch up to it again. It's right there, waiting for you to pick up where you fell off. Sure, the horses will be looking at you like you're a dumbass … but horses can be judgmental assholes so …

Everything is Relative

Before we get into the healing, I want to point out that every side has its own story, and it's not necessary for you to convince people to hear yours. My father had a succinct, albeit at the time insanely frustrating thing to hear, way of reframing his Perspective Cube lesson for in-the-moment attitude checks: "Everything is relative."

What he meant was that every story has a thread that connects it to your side and someone else's side, and the truth is simply a perception in between.

I've been re-taught this lesson over and over again through the trials, blunders, and miracles of my life. Sometimes through tears. But sometimes through absolute chaos and humor.

"You're Welcome!"

I fucking love waterslides. The woosh. The splash. The speed. Even the water that slams through your sinuses (much like the basketball *ping!* as it collides with your face) when you reach the pool at the bottom. I. Love. Them.

Well ... I love them *now*.

As would be the catalyst for many a physical injury in my life, on one fateful day in 1992, gravity would forsake me. You see, I was a wiry thing at six years old. But I never thought of myself as small because of my adorably round toddler-esque potbelly. So the lesson in physics I was to learn came as a complete kick in the face.

I *realllly* wish I didn't mean that literally.

Because I've always been too big for my britches in the most fabulous way, I selected the larger inner tube for this adventure. My 75-year-old great-grandfather, who was fit as a fiddle, had climbed the old White Water Park winding wooden staircase all the way to the top with me. He was so excited to "have my back" as he shooed me along to take on the slide first. "Don't worry, I'll be right behind you!"

I stepped into the little holding pond at the top of the slide, plopped my tiny butt in the center of the tube, and eagerly stared past my tiny little legs kicking excitedly as they flopped over the edge. I held the bar above my head and eagerly awaited the countdown to ensure I wouldn't collide with another slider. 3 ... 2 ...1 ... GO! I delivered a victorious "YAWP," let go of the bar, threw up the deuces, and ... didn't budge.

This absolutely should have been a warning to me and more so to the adults watching. Inspiring someone to swap my inner tube for the smaller option ... it did not. Instead it inspired the begrudging teenage employee to push me out of the corral with his foot. And with a squeal of elation from me, and the curl of a lip from him, I was off!

Woosh! Woosh! Woosh! The tiny beams of light peeking through the air holes of the completely dark enclosed slide were zinging past my face. I was enamored with the echo of my own voice and tried all different types of sounds. I pressed my toes down to see if I was grown enough to trace the bottom of the slide from the seat of my inflated throne. Stretch ... strettttttch. I did it! I touched the bottom! What a weird little victory!

But wait ... I'm still touching the bottom.

That was the moment I realized the shift in my weight had allowed the inner tube to rise just enough to wedge itself a few inches above the water. And tiny me ... too light to get the fucker moving again.

I laughed and tried my best to bronco buck myself loose. But the more I tried, the more I stayed. And then I heard it ... my great grandfather's distant, "Whoo-hoo!"s.

Oh Fuck!

There I was, like a stick bug flailing in a puddle, fully aware that a grown-ass man was barreling toward me. I resorted to screaming, "WAIT! I'M STUCK! YOU HAVE TO STOP!"

I know what you're thinking ... child genius, right? Well to my surprise, not only did he not heed my physically impossible instructions, but when he heard me his response was, "Ope! HOLD ON! I'M A-COMIN'!"

I could actually feel the take-charge attitude he jumped right into, which only ramped up my terror. I looked up and saw him swoosh around the corner like a man with a mission.

"No. No. No. No." I mustered.

With all too much excitement in his eyes, he yelled, "I'M GONNA POP YOU LOOSE!"

"Noooo. No. No." My eyes widened even further.

He straightened his legs and flexed his feet, forming a 75-year-old battering ram.

"WHAT?! NOOO!!!" I screamed.

Then with a *BLOOSH* of impact, my body was ejected. It bounced only once and landed a few feet ahead, free from the inner tube but still in the slide. Before I even knew to brace myself for a second collision, I heard yet another "OPE!" and with an echoing *SPLURMP* I was run over by my great-grandfather and his inner tube.

At this point, were a six-year-old to ever utter the words, "What the fuck?!" it would have been me, sputtering and choking on chlorine and the taste of my own blood.

But whether I actually vocalized the thought or not, it wouldn't have deterred the next and final phase in his mission to save me. And in that moment, with surprising dexterity and upper body strength, he flung his arm behind him, his trumpet-playing claws fully extended, and snatched me up by my long, wet, tangled hair. He shouted, "HOLD ON! I GOTCHYA!" as he dragged me, gargling water and curse words, face down the entire remainder of the slide.

When we reached the pool at the bottom, I jumped out of the water and screamed, "I could have died!!!"

To which he smiled, lifted his chest victoriously, and proclaimed, "I know! Aren't you glad I was there? ... YOU'RE WELCOME!"

That was the first moment I knew that two people really could see the exact same event from opposite ends of the universe. And that, simply because you feel needed and like the savior, at the end of the day it doesn't inherently make you either.

Taking a Step Down

You now know it's lonely at the top. Which means you've accepted that "the top" is a fucked-up place to choose to live. So let's take one step down the ladder. I promise ... you and everyone around you will be okay.

Everything you read here can't be unread, unseen, or unfelt, so each step down the rungs from now on will be from a choice you make to continue to change your patterns.

And you will. You will learn to recognize those patterns, build new patterns, and then when the old ones show up, you'll have a simple maneuver to get around them. The key to recovery is consistency, but I don't know a single living human who hasn't missed a rung or two and ate shit while trying to climb down a ladder. So don't be so hard on yourself in this process, okay?

CHAPTER TWO

GIVE THE
REINS

No one is going to get their shit together unless you stop pretending it's YOUR shit to hold.

IN THE LAST CHAPTER we talked about the major fears of People Pleasers, but the reality is, we exist in a constant state of fear that can be tied to one (or more) of hundreds of scenarios!

These fears are like obligation goblins—or what I like to call obligoblins. Obligoblins make you believe the craziest shit, and you run forward on those beliefs without questioning them or stopping to look them straight in the eye.

By the end of this chapter, you will be able to assess these fears, speak them out loud, feel them in the pit of your stomach, and then assess their validity.

Drop the Bomb: Surviving Your Own Apocalypse

In this exercise, you are going to work through the cathartic conversation waiting for you IN your fear and discover the lessons the ugly bits have to teach you about yourself. You will drill down to your worst-case scenario fear and then tackle it.

STEP ONE

There is one particular ongoing conflict in your world at this moment. The one that's draining the most energy, that's flopping your stomach when it interrupts your daily thoughts. It's something you haven't said—or done—for fear of the outcome. You're going to name that now and then follow me down the rabbit hole ...

In as few words as possible, what will happen if this conflict goes horribly wrong?

If that actually came to be, what would happen?

And if THAT came to be ... what would happen?

If you feel you could go even deeper with these fears, take out a blank sheet of paper and go as deep as you're being pulled to go.

Now you've come to the final answer. This is the basement-level crust of the molten lava earth. This is the face of the fear you will be continuing this practice with. It may be, "If I lose this job I'll be homeless" or "My grandchildren will DIE if I'm not in their lives" or "If I tell him I might be gay he will hate me" ... whatever it is, you WILL carry it into the next, bright, and beautiful phase of this practice.

STEP TWO

Sit now, with this fear, in this realness. Whether it's logical or not, FEAR can control you. FEAR can manipulate your better judgment to abandon your self-care. This fear is very real and needs the talking stick for a moment if you ever expect to silence it. (And we won't actually be silencing it, we'll be educating and calming it!)

Imagine a world where your ultimate fear determined above is reality. It has come to pass. Shit has hit the fan and it's all true. Imagine this life. Allow any emotions, anger, rage, tears, and GRIEF to flow like a cleansing river. Grieve the loss of loved ones, rage against the devastation of disappointing superiors, cry for the pain of rejection ... whatever needs to be felt, now is your time to release it at its fullest expression.

Sometimes the tears will be attached to a sadness based in the desire to unsee a truth or take something back. Amanda Ranae Goodall said it best: "Sometimes the most painful grief is just the physical manifestation of your sudden awareness of all the times you have wronged yourself." She couldn't be more right, and you're allowed to feel the sadness in the weight of all you've held on your shoulders for so long. All the times you've held your tongue when you didn't want to … all the times you've put yourself in a bad position. So no matter how gut-wrenching the feeling gets, allow yourself to feel the relief in the awakening of the new you, rather than just the loss of the old you.

Be with this release fully and for as long as it needs you. Don't shut it up. Don't placate your nervous system with deep breaths and eye wipes. Don't distract your raging mind with miscellaneous thoughts and excuses to "snap out of it." Allow the pain to be fully expressed, and be as loud, ugly, and messy as necessary. Scream, break shit, smear snot on your wrist. No one is judging you here in this apocalypse, and you have nothing left to lose.

The tide will calm on its own. Your breath will slow. Your muscles will shudder. Your eyes will open fully. Your mind will calm. In this place, subdued of its own accord, this is where we move into the final phase …

STEP THREE

You rebuild.

Zombie movies rarely include the beautiful rebuilding part of the story because it's not gut-wrenching (literally) enough to keep our attention. But this is YOUR apocalypse. So what does rebuilding look like for you?

Still sitting in the alternate reality where your worst fear has come to pass, post physical grieving, what are some incredible things that could grow from the rubble? Could your daughter (with no other choice) step into her true role as a capable ... perhaps INCREDIBLE mother and care for your grandchildren in a way that you never knew possible? Could slamming one career door force an exciting new one to open? Could you embrace your true sexuality and finally feel this beautiful thing called the human experience as richly as everyone else?

What are three beautiful things that could happen in the aftermath of YOUR apocalypse?

```

```

I could waste pages telling you it's not worth the energy to fear the worst possible outcome, because life actually WANTS to surprise you! But fear is real. So instead I'll say this ... in the end, nobody ever wants to imagine a world without them in it. But sometimes you HAVE to imagine a world without you to help you see what people really CAN do were you not killing yourself to control the outcome.

Yes … the world NEEDS you. But feel these words loud and clear … the world needs THE REAL YOU. Not the controlling, overthinking, manipulative, fearful you. Not the you who's afraid to do what he/she/they has to do to live a fulfilled, supported, authentic life. Not the you who sees the worst-case scenario as the only possible outcome.

The

Real

You.

STEP FOUR

Mourn yourself and your possible non-existence. Honor it. Celebrate your life. A mentor of mine once shared a "Samurai death celebration" technique with me. The paraphrased takeaway being that hundreds of years ago, before Samurais went into battle, they celebrated their deaths. They would hold an amazing funeral and cheer for themselves. They would celebrate the lives they led, because they knew they were going to die. They could then go into battle and give everything, because death was the worst thing that could happen, and they already accepted that. Do the same with your greatest fear and celebrate everything that could happen if it came to be.

Another element of this phase is to practice gratitude. And no, not in that "sit with a journal and list all the reasons you're a brat for not appreciating what you have and call it gratitude" way. Simply realize you're NOT dead today. Realize the last spin of your spiral is NOT happening and life is pretty fucking awesome. And you DO have the power to dismantle and disarm these illogical fears and call back the power to yourself.

Create a mantra for yourself! Did your self-doubt-hole just clench shut? It's okay! You actually never needed some guru to create them for you. Mantras we create for ourselves are so much more deeply impactful. Every. Single. Word. has an energetic attachment to your inner child and the growth they're craving from you. So don't be shy. You don't need a guru when you have YOU.

Practice building your own mantras with these easy bonus steps once you're done weathering your apocalypse:

1. Read out loud the three beautiful things you wrote in Step Three.
2. Imagine a sparkling diamond-like thread attached to each one, pulsating with the abundance, likeness, and energy of all three of these beautiful things.
3. Give that sparkling thread a voice. What IS this illuminating, humbling, uplifting likeness these beautiful things have in common?

Sometimes it's simply one word. Sometimes it's the most exquisite short sentence. No matter what it is, the words came from your energy, your love, your heart. And anytime you repeat them, you will be dropped back into that sobering moment of clarity.

Keep the Phone in the Locker Please

My mother had a hysterectomy and was on medical leave from her position as head nurse in an oncology office. It was over Mother's Day, so I whisked her away to an exquisite spa in the North Carolina Highlands for a weekend of relaxation.

Of course, she couldn't relax. We had to place our cell phones in lockers as we moved about the facility, but every time we went to the locker room, she rushed to check her messages. I could almost see her hair falling out in front of me as she complained that people from work were constantly calling and texting. "Where is this?" "Where is that?" "What's the code for blah blah blah?"

I could see her levels of stress, but she couldn't.

That evening, at the hotel, I sat her down and said, "It's shockingly unprofessional for them to be contacting you while you are on medical leave. Not to mention putting you at risk every time you answer. You will be held responsible for the information you're providing them, and your ass will be the first one under that bus if everything goes tits up anyway."

She scoffed and threw her hands up. "What am I supposed to do? I'm not THERE to fix it!"

I winced and said, "Honestly, Mom, what is the worst thing that would happen if you don't answer?"

Without hesitation, and in the most flabbergasted tone she barked back, "They could fire me!"

I couldn't hold back the chuckle. "Mom! You and I both know that's illegal."

She raised her eyebrows and pursed her lips in protest.

"Wait ... You DO know that ... don't you?"

Her still-panicked face said all I needed to know.

"I know just what we need to do ..."

I walked her through her own Drop the Bomb spiral. At the bottom, she had a fear that the office would suffer. More than being fired. More than being held accountable. She feared the staff would be sitting there, incompetent with their dicks in their hands, while the patients suffered.

I told her to picture herself in a world where she died today.

Of course, her first reaction was complete and utter offense.

I told her to bear with me. Picture it. "Now what is that office doing? Are the doors going to open tomorrow if you die today?"

She looked hurt and uncomfortable but said, "Yes, they would still open their doors."

I nodded. "They'd figure it THE FUCK OUT! Right??"

It took a moment and then she agreed. "If I was actually dead, they'd be fine. So why am I worried that just because I'm not there, I have to answer all these messages?"

She had a wonderful moment of clarity, and together we wrote the very simple text response, "I am on medical leave. Direct any further questions to your immediate supervisor. I will no longer be answering my phone."

She then turned off her phone and was a new woman for the next three days!

Consoling Your Inner Child

When you've had some time to digest this exercise, you'll hopefully have an initial sense of, "Oh okay, so I can be completely driven by a pathological fear that I know logically doesn't make sense, but that actually drives my actions."

Realize that your fear is like a child. Children can be ridiculous and over the top. They can scream their asses off about something that makes no sense. But if you take the time to stop, get on their level, look them in the eye, and ask, "Hey, buddy, what's actually going on?" you'll most likely find there is truly something to be addressed.

Once you know a wailing child is just hungry, your pit of anxiety eases and you can find them something to eat. You can listen, give their fear a voice, and honor it.

Your obligoblin is the same. Once you've worked through the exercise and gotten to the bottom of the spiral, when you face your fear … it will have changed. Instead of being terrifying, it will have an innocent, child-like quality. It will feel like a scared child telling you their fears, and you will know they aren't true.

Any time you change a fear into what it really is— which is your inner child throwing a temper tantrum and feeling unsafe—you flip the script, see the fear for its pure essence, and are then open to absorbing the lesson you needed to learn. Imagine a child sobbing hysterically, telling you that the sky is going to fall. You know the sky isn't going to fall, but you switch into the caregiver role, comfort them, and tell them, "I know I'm not a scientist. I can't prove to you that the sky won't fall, but try to trust me."

This role of caregiver empowers you. This innocent person trusts you with their fear and wants you to make it better. This beautiful feeling can be had with your own fear, when you respect it enough to look it in the face and see what the hell it's screaming about.

Don't Ignore Your Fears

Unfortunately, we exist in a society that peddles in toxic positivity. *If you don't look at something, if you don't know about it, and if you pour every ounce of energy into a positive way of thought, everything will improve, and your fears will go away.*

Pure. Adulterated. Bullshit.

If you ignore your fear, it just gets louder and more ridiculous! If you don't pay attention to it, your subconscious damn well will. And then it will sit there and make up some irrational, illogical, destructive narrative that will drive you in your physical body, your emotions, and your energy.

There's a part of your brain that knows this is nonsensical, but that makes the fear even more real.

So instead, pause. Work through the exercise above and reflect on it. You won't release this fear today. That's okay. Rather, you will expose the spiral. Every time you practice this, every time you get that pit in your stomach, pause and dig deeper. Think to yourself, "I may not be able to dismantle this fear in this moment, but I can disarm the spiral." Give your obligoblin a name and look it in the face. Just like you, it craves to be seen and understood.

The Fall of The Phoenix

When I first developed the PPA type quiz, my incredibly supportive mother was more than happy to take it. To my surprise, she popped into my online group and declared "I'm not just A Phoenix ... I'm THE Phoenix." Truer words have probably never been spoken from a mother to a daughter. I wasn't sure if she fully understood the levity of having an archetype modeled after her.

She waltzed through the four-day beta sampling of the first recovery program I was creating, and connected with the material just enough to acknowledge how awful this addiction feels for us all, while holding her own recovery at arm's length behind the smirk of "easier said than done, honey," "that's so great that this works ... for you!" and "maybe one day!"

It wasn't uncommon, when asking my mother how she was feeling, to receive the (only partially) kidding, "I feel like I've been hit by a Mack Truck!" It wasn't uncommon to find her, no matter the job, in tears of frustration and feeling overwhelmed. It wasn't uncommon for our phone calls to begin with a list of all that she had accomplished so far that day, only to be then cut short with a list of all the things she still needed to get done. It wasn't uncommon for her to become visibly anxious when invited to something, anything, by anyone, if it wasn't already accounted for in her schedule.

This was simply the mom I grew up loving and had all but accepted.

As a child I knew no better, and I thought that's what life was meant to be. Give of yourself, no matter the cost. As I grew older, I ignored my own manifestation of this addiction and simply became detached. I tried to take her anxieties and tears with a grain of salt ... after all, how much salt does it take for an addict to finally change their situation? Then I began my recovery and started to really see it.

I saw how isolated she had become in her urgency to control the uncontrollable. I saw how she had betrayed her own energy to ultimately feel validated, affirmed, liked, and loved.

One year, I went home for Thanksgiving. My mother spent a beautiful day on her farm excitedly showing me the renovations and new animal additions.

Afterward, I washed up and was getting ready for the evening in the downstairs bedroom, when there was a knock at the door.

"Your sister and I were just talking about the house and the property ...," she said with a pause.

"I was thinking of buying the acreage behind me ..."

"Ok?" I responded before adding coyly, "I think that's awesome! But that's not something you need my approval for."

She looked taken aback but continued. "Well of course your opinion matters, when I die—"

Rudely, but involuntarily, I interrupted her. "Nope! Nooo, no, no. Don't do anything with this property for ME. If you left it to me, I would honestly sell my half to Katrina, and if she wasn't interested, we would sell the property together. But no future version of my life includes a farm. I support anything you're doing for your enjoyment of it now, but please don't say you're doing it FOR me."

Immediately came the devastated, frustrated tears. I felt horrible at the sight of them, but I couldn't lie to placate her. I no longer entertained that side of my addiction. And as much as she hid her exhaustion of running the farm, it came in frequently occurring and overflowing waves.

Nope, I couldn't allow myself to be the reason behind that exhaustion.

Attached to an expression I could only read as hurt induced by her ungrateful daughter's audacity, she returned upstairs to cook the turkey.

My sister and I finally joined her in the kitchen where she was engaging in a high-anxiety talk about her workplace with her boyfriend at the time, Sir Douchenozzle Mcgee.

"I DON'T HAVE A CHOICE, THEY'LL FIRE ME!"

She was speaking of the office rule restricting employees from using the customer parking lot and instead forcing them to use a satellite lot across the one-lane street and up the hill. All in a rural town, with no sidewalks, no light posts, no crosswalks, and no shoulder. Just dark mountain curves, blind corners, and a steep drop-off on either side.

Despite the employees addressing administration about their safety concerns, the rule was still enforced.

She had almost been struck the evening prior while walking on the "correct" side of the road, and she was still fuming.

We had interrupted the part of the conversation where my mother was convincing herself, while sprinkling mini marshmallows over the sweet potato casserole, that she would just have to walk on the "other" side of the road.

"Someone's going to get hit, and they'll say it's our fault, but what are we supposed to do? If we park in the lot, we'll be written up. So either I take the chance, or I lose my job!"

My sister and I exchanged a look only sisters fueled with concern and desperation can, and we knew we had to get through to her before she People Pleased herself into an early grave.

We took her aside and I asked her very seriously, "Mom? Like, no shit ... what would happen to you if you got fired?"

She rolled her eyes and scoffed. She was still obviously annoyed with me, so I let my sister take the wheel. "No really, Mom, what would happen?"

"I would lose the house, I wouldn't be able to afford my life insurance premiums, I would lose everything. I can't keep this up without that income."

She went on to list very specifically the spiral that would occur. It was such an isolated, heartbreaking spiral, and in that moment, we could really feel how unsupported she felt. Not just hear it and be annoyed by it because WE knew how untrue it was—but FEEL it. And in an instant, Katrina and I took a deep breath and in unison shifted our perspective with audible "ohhhh"s.

"Do you actually think we would LET any of that happen to you?"

Mom began to cry. "I would never burden you like that, you're my babies, I'm supposed to always have a place for YOU to run home to if YOU need it."

I braved the chance of her not hearing my words out of any holdover "meh" she may have felt about our earlier interaction, but I had to say them. "We need you, Mom."

"I KNOW! That's what I'm sayi---"

"No, mom. We need you ALIVE."

She looked up at us and froze.

"Do you think we want to inherit a farm after our mother had a heart attack just from the upkeep? Do you think we want a life insurance policy cashed in after our mother was hit by a fucking truck just trying to keep the job that paid for it? We need you. And whatever we need to do to help you stay here, happy, and healthy—we will do it."

And there she was. The mom I always saw as superwoman strong, sobbing in the Eeyore onesie we had gotten her for Christmas the year before. Exhausted and ashamed. But most importantly, visibly relieved.

As we continued on, so much weight was lifted from the room I swear even the color changed.

We had an eye-opening conversation about her responsibilities, about the life she had created around her, and asked if the pressure was all really worth it.

"Sometimes I imagine what a life without all these responsibilities could look like, what it would feel like to not always be drowning," she said with a refreshing hope gleaming in her eyes.

We had an amazing rest of our holiday, invoking all the awesome things this life could give her were SHE to become a priority.

But as with any addiction, the ah-ha moments and the outpouring of love and support from others won't stick if you're not ready.

And she wasn't ready.

Much like the relief she felt after our Drop the Bomb practice at the spa, it was short lived. Because outside of those would-be life-changing moments, she was refusing to look her fear, her Addiction, in the face.

And the very next fall, while walking to her car after clocking out for the evening, the Universe whispered, "If you won't change, I'll make you change."

And with that, she was hit from behind by a Mack garbage truck. Struck directly in the back of the head.

She survived. Of course she did; somewhere in there was still a superwoman, after all.

But her life changed. It had to. Her boyfriend of nine years broke up with her because he said she and her farm were too much responsibility. She loved her animals, but it became too much. We sold the farm, for 100k more than was owed on it, and as I write these words, she is on long-term disability while my sister and I fill the financial holes until she is able to begin the next chapter of her life.

SHE changed after that, and not just because of the brain injury. Her fear of people showing their true colors came to fruition, but she survived. She began speaking up for herself in ways she never had. She began trying on new, different identities. She is light and free. Even in the times I don't agree with her, or the new versions of her she is discovering, a big part of my heart will always be happy that she's finally living a life on HER terms.

I wrote this special quote just for her, lest she forget that shit ...

"All the positive life changes a Pleasing Addict will avoid in the name of 'self-sacrifice' will never fool The Universe, Your Higher Power, or God."

Ask for Help

This isn't a request. It's a fact. You have to ask for help. When nothing makes sense, when you haven't figured it all out, this is the time to ask for help. As a People Pleaser, we don't ask for help until we know exactly how someone can help us. That can be very isolating and only serves to exacerbate the problem you're going through. You may not want to look stupid, or vulnerable, but your fear spirals can be knocked off track before they get bad—just by you asking for help and refusing to drown.

Allow the world to prove you wrong. Pleasers have that faux-value system we talked about earlier that they constantly maintain. The people they are intimidated by are the few people they view as higher value than themselves. And the things they do best are the things they are most in conflict over. You are the best at loving, which is why it's fine that your loved one doesn't do as much. You're just better at it, you choose to suffer, and it's fine. The value system only leads to exhaustion.

You want everyone to do their own work. You want to be loved as much as you love. But you don't give anyone a chance to. And your deepest fear typically has to do with someone else's inability to succeed. You don't even give them a chance. But you have to stop trying to prove you are better and let go of the fear such that they can actually step up and prove just how capable they are.

So ask for help. You need to allow someone the chance to prove you wrong.

CHAPTER THREE

REALITY
CHECK

*Friendly reminder from your throat
chakra: the SUCCESS of your
communication is NOT measured
by the OUTCOME*

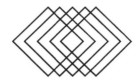

YOU ARE RESPONSIBLE for 100 percent of your experiences.

I'm sure you don't want to hear that. You probably don't believe it. You are probably sorting through the most horrific experiences that have ever happened to you and those closest to you. Perhaps the first thing that comes to mind to prove me wrong is your college roommate who was raped. And you're internally yelling at me, saying, "Are you honestly telling me it was THEIR fault?"

God, NO. Of course not. What happened was not their fault. They weren't asking for it. The things that happen to you aren't because you deserve them.

What I'm saying is that your experience around any event is 100 percent your responsibility. Your LIFE is your responsibility. Your healing from the event is 100 percent your responsibility.

I get it. I know it's totally not fair that you have to be responsible for fixing the damage that other people have inflicted upon you.

Unfortunately, life isn't fair.

Instead, life is fucking amazing and complicated.

I know you may need to sit with this concept for a bit, but it's important that you absorb it and can accept that you have full control over how you deal with the aftermath of situations. This understanding is the only way you can move forward to healing your People Pleasing Addiction.

This isn't to say that shifting your pain and healing your trauma is a light switch that you control. But your dedication to your healing, and the permission you grant yourself to seek out and get the help you deserve ... that, my dear, is all on you.

Mama Bear

Catherine was alone. She had been abandoned by everyone. Everyone who knew who she used to be. All those who had her back through life ... even her attacker.

What kind of world was this where she was left to clean up the shattered pieces from someone else's destruction? Where no matter how much someone wanted to help, they couldn't? Where there was no possible way to confront her attacker to find answers or gain even a glimmer of hope that he could fully understand the damage he had caused her heart, her blood, her bones, and her soul? Where no matter how many exits are clearly marked in a room, her survival is unfairly in her hands, and the number of doors will never be a guarantee that she will run fast enough ... not if, but when, the moment comes?

Catherine, a psychiatrist, had fallen in love with a "broken man," sure! But she thought she could heal him. And what kind of world would make it possible for her to heal anyone but the one she cherished most? And then ... what kind of world would make her responsible for fixing all that someone else had broken? What kind of world would let HER feel broken for defending herself?

Often, he had vaguely spoken about a "plan," a secret grand design he felt he was a part of. It was never a clear warning of what was to horrifically come, but rather a fog. A mere hint of the danger he was truly in.

She never felt the danger was hers. She trusted him. She loved him. She thought she could fix him.

Until that night, when she walked through her front door to a life that would never again be the same.

Her pets were slaughtered, their bodies left to set the stage. There, her lover, a confidant and now a murderer stood. After all he'd taken, there was still one final demand of her that glared from his eyes as he charged her.

The demand to complete his grand design.

For her to kill him.

With everything tearing apart inside of her and no other choice, she took his life to save her own.

Catherine came to me a few weeks later, isolated, questioning her own existence in such a cruel world. How could someone select, no ... fucking hand pick, a human to do this? Why was SHE his final puzzle piece? What had he gotten her into karmically? Would God ever forgive her?

Since that fucked up but fateful night, she had been having recurring dreams of a bear. A giant, menacing grizzly bear. She was hiking with her deceased lover as if nothing had yet transpired. And then the bear disrupted their path. Not attacking, simply reclaiming its space as it walked along. She was flooded with terror, worried he or the dogs would be attacked. The bear managed, with its domineering stride and knowing presence, to create distance between her and her lover. She shouted to clear the others out of the bear's path but felt a deep sense of understanding once the initial fear faded.

For some time she believed the dreams were a cruel joke. A revisiting of the terror and a "too little too late" warning of what was to come.

But in her waking moments, she was determined to work, to truly look into this bear's eyes and find its meaning, to find herself again through therapy and emotional development.

I asked if she had ever heard of the calm, but menacing grizzly's presence in a dream as signifying the dreamer's own maternal reclamation soon to follow?

She went silent for a moment...

Then released the sweetest, most cleansing cry.

Once she gathered herself enough to speak, her voice resonated with pure, unadulterated, unfuckwithable knowing.

"It was me! The bear was me! It was me all along! ... Oh. My. God ...

... IT'S STILL ME!"

With those three words, she walked away from the guilt, the fear, the shame, and the unknowing. Will she stumble upon them in the future? Of course. Trauma isn't repaired in a single phone call. Or with a single awareness. But in that moment,

Catherine put down the box of WHAT THE FUCK her attacker had all but glued to her chest and reclaimed her autonomy. In that moment, Mama Bear took inventory of what was left of her life. She sat, like the cosmic fucking force she is, in the duality of knowing what happened to her holds 0 percent of her responsibility, while declaring that she is 100 percent responsible for what she does with it (the trauma, the reality, and her LIFE) from here on out.

The Need to be LOVED

We continue to talk about fears, and the People Pleasers I've worked with are consistently afraid of losing their otherworldly ability to love so deeply. They know they need to change because they are hurting themselves, but there's a part of themselves and the situation they can't let go of. The part that says, "I LOVE how much I love. I LOVE how much I care about the people around me. I LOVE how much effort I put into things. I don't ever want to let that go or believe it's wrong to feel this way."

Here's the thing. You don't have to let go of ANY of this. My branding of the "Whimsical Rebel" was born of the belief that you can still be this ridiculous, amazing, glowing ball of whimsy and love without damaging yourself in the process.

The problem was never with how much they love. It lies in the Pleaser's view of love itself. They confuse feelings of adoration and gratitude from others as love. What's worse, they view the perceived reception of those feelings, even when they're not actually given. A Pleaser can hyper-rationalize their way out of feelings of rejection by using the joy they felt when creating and delivering their gift of love. It felt so good to give the love that, "It's OK if I don't get it back, it made me happy to do it." Which is cute … until it's used as a surrogate for truly receiving love in return.

Believe it or not, feeling needed by another human isn't love. Feeling needed is feeling needed.

Why do you mistake the two? Because on a crust-of-the-earth level, you actually think you're not deserving of the epic love you give to others. So you manipulate others into giving you the *feeling* of love.

And for us, it's the feeling of being needed.

I know, that may be icky to read. But it's true. Think about all the times you've gone above and beyond in the hopes of getting validation in return. (Even when you've cleverly told yourself that wasn't your intent.)

That, my friend, is manipulation.

Changing Your Perception of Love

You may be triggered into rolling your eyes, slapping this book down on the coffee table, and busying yourself

with the mundane: dishes, escapism, or simply returning to your day. But hopefully a little bit of this starts to
seep in. I hope it questions what you consider to be love.
'Cause shit! You've been trained to believe that love is
a pat on the head! Love is an affirmation that someone
can't live without you!

So, it makes sense that you're scared of the aftermath.
If your idea of love changes, what is left? It's hard to imagine a love better than the love you've been trained to feel.

The cure to this fear is to tap into the gorgeous, opti-
mistic, whimsical part of yourself. Start believing that
everything's going to be fine. You can fix anything, and
there's a reality where your future will be better than you
even thought possible! When you start to derail, lean
hard into your excitement and hope. Think about what
you would tell someone else in this situation.

Understand there isn't going to be a void in the love
you feel and receive just by changing your perception of
it. You don't have to exist in a state of lovelessness. The
dopamine hits you received in your current version of
love—the validation, manipulation, and pain—will be
slowly replaced by your own self-love and validation.

When you start to feel that self-love, that's when you
will start to feel the love from others rather than manipulate a manufactured version of love out of them.

The process is a slow replacement, and you won't
even feel it. I promise that you won't be sitting there

emotionally alone with your heart bleeding in your hand. You will still love just as hard, but you won't supplement your efforts with your own energy and self-respect. You won't love out of sacrifice. And you'll find that you can love so much more beautifully when you're not tainted with self-deprecation.

Two Years of Atonement

Precisely one year before I left my ex-husband, I warned him. Through my tears and brokenness, I mustered what little courage I had to speak up for my needs and said, "I married YOU, not your father, but I see you becoming him more and more. I'm too in love with you to leave, but one day your indifference won't hurt my feelings anymore. One day you won't be able to make me cry. And on that day, I promise you, I'll leave."

His response, whether it was lackadaisical or endearing, wasn't potent enough to file away. The memory of this conversation sits in my mind like a one-sided argument with a mirror. And it should. Every single day we choose for ourselves the level of suffering we are willing to endure. The promise I made that night was more for me than for him.

I spent the rest of the night with my bestie, Kelley. My tears were dried and tucked deep into my heart pocket by the time I turned up on her porch with a magnum of Pinot Grigio and Chinese take-out. We bitched about our men, being careful to skirt the truth of our own culpability in settling for our respective levels of suffering. The next day we would wake up in the same loop, with the same problems, and continue with our lives as if nothing was worth changing ... yet.

Ten months later I harmlessly met Derren. And for the two months following, I ignored my obvious emotional connection with Derren and in turn ignored the giant dead horse that was my marriage. But a single phone call would change everything.

I needed to return to Atlanta for the funeral of a family friend, and my soon-to-be ex-husband declined to go, what with his heavy responsibilities to his online role-playing guild and his distaste for what would assuredly turn into an evening of karaoke. After the funeral, I said goodbye to dear friends and met Derren for a beer.

I excused myself to use the bathroom, and while I was perched on the toilet, my phone rang. I answered the call from my husband mid-stream. I giggled as you do when you've had a few and you're the only one who knows your pants are around your ankles ...

It clearly annoyed him. "What are you doing?" Acid dripped from his voice.

"Ummm ... I'm peeing." I was suddenly confused and wondering why I was in trouble.

The call continued with vitriol about nothing in particular, and suddenly there I was again ... arguing with my indignant reflection in an imaginary mirror.

"Huh!" I interrupted.

"Huh, what?" he demanded sharply.

"Well, normally when you're like this, I end up crying. This time I'm not!" I admittedly was probably over enthusiastic, almost like I expected him to be equally as thrilled about this sudden gift of detachment from the emotional pain I was used to experiencing.

He was not thrilled, but it didn't matter. I told him I was going to hang up and did just that.

The next day I didn't want to come home. Something had shifted, and I felt like only sadness waited for me. I texted my husband and he asked when I would be returning. I responded, "I don't know," with no explanation, no apology, no preface. It felt SO liberating. I couldn't figure out why until I remembered my promise a year prior. This was now that breaking point, and the moment I made up my mind.

I wasn't the only one who felt the shift. That night Derren kissed me. I stopped him for only a moment, almost as an involuntary sign of respect while standing over the grave of my marriage. We made love. I had my first penetrative orgasm. I regretted nothing. And while tracing my fingers through his chest hair, I whispered a final sentiment of full detachment.

"Poor guy."

I rolled over, grabbed my phone, composed a text, hit send, hit the mute button, and went to sleep. After seven years of losing myself, seven years of trying to help someone be better than they wanted to be, seven years of teaching someone how to love me and being told I was too hard to love, I stopped standing my ground and simply turned and walked the fuck away.

"I don't know when I'm coming home, but when I do it won't be as your wife. I love you, but it's over."

That night I had the best sleep of my life.

The next day wasn't so great. Every relationship would cease to exist as I knew it. It was a People Pleaser's nightmare. Friends were hurt. Relatives demanded explanations. All my loved ones seemed to feel betrayed by the lack of forewarning.

By the end of the day, I was exhausted. I never for a moment wished I had done things any differently, but I simply had to endure the penance for having put myself first.

I finally answered the last text, put down the phone, and looked at Derren, who never left my side. Before I could collapse into a useless "just feed and pet me" blob, the phone lit up. With a weary heart, I resumed my defense position on the edge of the bed and prepared to explain myself yet again, but what I read made me drop the phone. In that moment I cried my first tears.

Derren grabbed the phone, thinking he would find something horrific, but instead he found a single text from Kelley.

"I'm about to cry. I'm just SO PROUD OF YOU. I know no one has noticed because y'all always seemed so happy, and I know you weren't faking it. But I saw. And it broke my heart watching you just go through the motions when you're meant to be, and have, so much more."

I felt so seen, understood, and accepted during what others believed should have been the most shameful point in my life.

Derren turned the phone off and curled up behind me. He wrapped his massive bear paws around me and whispered, "Wow, now that's a true friend. I can't wait to meet her, and anyone else you feel deserves to stay in our lives."

I wish I could say the perfect ending to that day was enough to rip the aching need to be liked and loved from the bottom of my stomach and cast it into a 50-foot hole for all eternity. But that's not how addictions work.

Half my brain twirled on a hilltop with new-found confidence and strength, like Julie Andrews. I heard my inner child. I HEARD HER. And I mustered up the strength to answer her, despite the commotion it would cause, despite the loved ones I would lose in the battle.

But the other half of my brain said, "Yeah, but I can fix this, and everyone can still be ok. Hold my beer!"

And for two years I paid the price. I remained closely entangled with my ex-husband's progress as we stayed "friends." I truly believed I was helping him through our divorce. I let him scream at me if he had a bad day. I let him disrespect me to our friends. I gave him dating advice. I even went as far as to take on every last cent of debt we had acquired. Finally I realized I was creating further damage for us both, and I severed communication entirely.

> For two years I atoned for my sin.
> The sin wasn't adultery.
> The sin was whoring myself out for someone else's emotional recovery while abandoning my own.

You Don't Need Validation

I wasn't innocent in all of it. My need to control our relationship wasn't birthed from the ending of it. I tried to control my ex-husband's perception of me for seven years. Was I completely to blame for his growing complacency and emotional distancing? Ew, no. But denying him the opportunity to organically love the real me definitely had a part to play, like a side dish of emasculation to accompany an already shitty meal. But guess what? You can't allow someone to love you by existing in a place of equality while simultaneously fully believing you can control their perception of you.

It doesn't work.

People Pleasers are taught that love is validation, and they can be validated for slowly killing themselves for someone's benefit. The validation makes the sacrifice worth it (except now we know it doesn't), and a platform for that validation is a manipulation and control of other people's perceptions of us.

If you can control what everyone thinks of you, then you can control your drug supply. You can control how everyone around you makes you feel. And then maybe you can control life. And then maybe you can control the uncontrollable. And then maybe no one you love will die ...

You see how the fears continue to spiral? And it all starts with the simple idea that you could actually control another human's perception of you.

My Awful Laugh

2010 was a beast of a year that both cemented and crumbled my confidence over and over again. During the week I worked the night shift and busted out overtime on the "reg" in an Aiken, South Carolina ICU/PCU as a Unit Secretary and Telemetry Tech.

Most mornings I would climb into bed alone, the sheets still warm with the scent of Derren having just left for his normy day job. Three or four 12-hour night shifts a week left little time to have a life. But the weekends? Those were for my soul.

I'd clock out at 7:00 a.m. Friday morning, hit the gym, and then head home with just enough time for some emotional re-up sex and to pack my shit. Then I was off to Murphy, North Carolina, to play piano and sing at any bar that would have me. This was where my family, friends, peers, and most importantly to my 25-year-old ego ... my FANS were waiting. Because on the weekends? On the weekends Ahdri Kent was a goddamn ROCKSTAR.

Sure, it was a small mountain town and I never strayed further. But for my Self-Sabotaging ass it was perfect. I never had to grow. They loved me, night after night, for doing what I did best and never thinking any bigger.

Until one night they didn't. And I was served my first dose of haterade.

It wasn't even haterade honestly, it was from a dear friend that to this day I consider a wonderful human being. But my deep-seeded need to be liked and loved hadn't even begun to be unwound at this point, and this would be a shock to my fragile, popular heart.

It happened one night partying after a performance.

Jon, the Ginger Gentleman, was a kind, hard-working, loyal friend of Jess's who, after many a night at my shows, and drinking afterward, would become my friend as well.

But not that night.

Jon and his girlfriend had retired for the evening, as they had a baby shower to attend the next morning. Jess, Ronnie, and I stayed up late playing dominos and chatting. Around 4:00 a.m., during a particularly funny turn of Jess's, we all let out a laugh.

In that moment, mid cackle, the bedroom door swung open violently, and Jon began collecting his belongings from around the living room.

We immediately thought there must have been a romantic tussle and he was leaving his girlfriend after a spicy argument! Or maybe he'd received terrible news and was on his way to sort it out! Whatever the reason for his outburst, we were concerned for his safety.

"Dude, what's wrong?" I asked.

"Nothing." He sat on the armchair across from me and put his shoes on.

"Then why do you look so pissed?" Ronnie asked.

"I'm not, just leave it alone." He grabbed his keys from the end table.

"Where the fuck do you think you're going?" Jess asked.

"Home." He stood to leave.

"THE FUCK YOU ARE!" We all demanded he put his keys down, knowing he was in no shape to drive in the first place, let alone as upset as he was.

"Fine!" He sat, more frustrated than before.

Jess begged, "Jon, what the hell, man. You're freakin' me out and it's about to piss me off! Tell us what's wrong!"

"Please don't make me say it." He leaned forward, slapped his hands on his knees, and adopted the defiant "I warned you" expression. Then with a solitary point of a fed-the-fuck-up finger, he said, "IT'S HER!"

I shit you not, I looked behind me. Nope no one there.

"ME?!"

"HER!?"

"AHDRI?!"

"YES! HER! Her fucking LAUGH! It's SO goddamn loud! And it's not JUST loud, it's shrieky! It's like she's actually screaming! Every time I close my fuckin' eyes, it's like someone throws a cat against the wall and it scares me awake!"

I had never given a second thought to it! The volume, the timbre, none of it. It was the unsolicited sound of pure joy.

I froze. A friend, a fan, a good human being was just dripping an acidic lack of love for me. Enough to voice it all out loud. Enough to cause a physical rage. This challenged everything I was ever taught about being admired, maintaining loyalty, and

SECURING love and affection. You know ... all the lies that create the foundation of People Pleasing Addiction.

My anxiety ebbed when I realized I wasn't the only one shocked into speechlessness. We all sat in tense silence until Ronnie took the words right out of my mouth with the most smartass look I've ever seen his face wear. "Wowwww, sorry her joy offends you so much, bro."

Jon shot Ronnie the saddest look, realizing in that moment that he may have hurt my feelings.

Jess and I gave Jon about two seconds to back-pedal, but before he could get out the first, "No, I'm sorry, it's not like THAT. It's just..." we died laughing. For a solid ten minutes we reveled in the ridiculousness that had taken place. Even Jon began laughing and apologized for how out of character his outburst had been. He hugged me. "I'm so sorry, dude! I promise, any other time I really do LOVE the way you laugh!"

But nothing was going to delete the impact of someone bringing a party to a full halt, singling me out, and spitting the unfathomable claim that my laugh was the bane of their current existence.

It hurt in the weirdest way. And my ego wouldn't forget it. I even used it as a way to turn the focus from me onstage when, for months thereafter, every time he sauntered into my shows, I would pause the set, point him out to the crowd, and regale them with the story of how my laughter can bring a grown man to his knees.

You Can't Predict the Future

We often excuse our manipulation by relying on our *psychic ability*. You think you know what someone else is going to say, so you sit in the car and have an hour-long, fake conversation in your head before you go inside and converse with the living human being that you should be talking to. You coach and try to fix someone, rather than being present and listening to what someone has to say.

You engage in this value system where you know what's best. You know how to fix something. You know how to word conflict so the other party will see it your way. You know how to manipulate, but it never *feels* like manipulation. It feels like, "I just know how they react to things, and I don't want to trigger them."

When you sit and manipulate people's reactions to you, you are completely robbing them of the ability to respond organically. You may think you know the best outcome and try to lean into it, but guess what? You don't. You will never know what the best outcome is going to be for you until it happens, and by wasting energy trying to wrap something in a bow to create your best outcome, you might be biting yourself in the ass ... and NOT in the sexy way.

Let's say you need to have a hard conversation with your loved one and you're scared they'll lose their shit. The best outcome would be NOT that, so you make sacrifices in your relationship. You ignore what's happening. But, perhaps, the best thing that could happen is you say what you're feeling, and you allow your partner to respond organically. Even if the result is a huge fight, maybe ... just maybe ... that fight is the best thing that could happen to both of you.

Stop trying to premeditate outcomes, and acknowledge that YOU don't have the clarity and insight yet to even know what the "best" outcome would be. Admit you are premeditating to achieve the most "comfortable" outcome, despite the continued devastation it may cause beneath the surface.

The best and only way to ensure you get a best outcome is to be honest, organic, and stop robbing your loved ones of the ability to be organic in return.

You're Not a Parrot Trainer

Don't confuse communication with manipulation. Some people can successfully manipulate a conversation to their perceived best interest and thus believe they are excellent at communicating.

No. Nope. Nah.

You are just excellent at manipulating your counter-part into acting like a parrot saying what you want them to say.

The measure of success in your communication isn't the outcome; rather, it's organically speaking from the heart and then allowing the other person to respond and not read from the script you present them.

Just like any addict, everyone around you becomes a puppet in getting you your desired effect. Your loved ones, your relatives, your grandparents, your parents, your children, your friends—they are all vessels for you to feel good, for you to dip into and get what you need out of them.

Meanwhile, the uncontrollable continues to grow in the background. You pretend it doesn't exist because you become so used to being able to control how you feel by just dipping into these little pots with different faces to get your fix, validation, and love. So the rest of the world continues to spin, and you become very good at ignoring how to behave and how to survive real life shit.

None of this was fun for me to discover about myself either. So if you're still turning these pages, I applaud you!

Dissolving the Value System

When you find comfort in this false reality, it often feels like you're a walking juxtaposition. You exist in a false value system where you place yourself on top and everyone else underneath. They *need* your love. They *need* you to do things right. They *need* you to take over.

The value system is a complete LIE. It's created by whatever the source may be for your personal Pleasing Addiction and validated one step at a time by your actions and successful pleasing manipulations. And it's ultimately mandated by you that you always have to be higher than everyone else.

Pitbulls especially imagine they can always do things better—even when watching an expert give a presentation, sing a song, or prepare food in the kitchen. The underlying manipulation never stops churning as it tries to make them feel accepted and on top. The Phoenix goes into heavy critique mode and always has something to say, even to their own detriment. They will even accidentally insult someone. Mice are very sweet and think they live under the radar, but they simultaneously attempt to control everyone's perception of them as the gracious caretaker.

"I can say the thing that I need to say for you to think I'm the person I want you to think that I am. And meanwhile, I can convince myself that I think we're all equal," said every Pleaser's subconscious ever.

It's just not possible to coexist in this space. You can't think that everyone's equal and doing the best they can—but also think you're the only person who can do the job right. It's a conflict, and when you exist in this conflict, it strips you of your identity. It strips you of all elements that can bring some sense of security to your life.

Visualize this. You are standing in a circle and your lover is in front of you. The circle is your relationship, and you both need to be inside of it. You, as a People Pleaser, take up so much space in that circle, trying to control every element of the relationship, that you force your lover out. You want them to take half the responsibility, but you are literally creating a force field and not allowing them in!

If someone loves you, they want to show up for you, and you have to learn to let them.

Fighting the Obligoblin

Your obligoblin survives on your value system. If you allow anyone to prove you wrong or step up and show that they are capable of—or God forbid better than you at—doing something you can do, your addiction fails to get the attention it needs.

Your brain will continue to fight for this addiction. Because if it goes away, what do you have? Your survival patterns are the counterpart of the addiction, as it helps remove some of the sense of impending doom.

Whenever possible, recognize that this is just a fucked-up behavioral problem, but it's not YOUR fucked-up problem. It's your addiction's problem. Separate yourself.

Comfort and ease aren't necessarily negative or something to avoid; rather, they are elements to recognize. There are some days that you need comfort—and that's okay! You don't need to always live in a space of analysis and being primed for change.

However, you need to recognize that you can't find comfort in manipulation. It causes the opposite and only serves to create more discomfort. You can only trick yourself for so long. Even when people do what you want them to do, you use a lot of hyper-aware, anxious, negative energy to manipulate them into doing it. You wear a disguise and take on their energy. You premeditate your words and mold them. You even stifle your own thoughts in the process.

Exposing Hidden Agendas

Hidden agendas are the super-gross underbelly of good deeds. Remember my story from the introduction about the unbuyable birthday gift, when I created the lists in my head of all the things I had done? Nobody wants to admit that they track all their good deeds, but all People Pleasers do.

Don't get me wrong. It's not in a McScrooge kind of way. We don't want to be paid back. We just want to keep track in case anyone calls into question our carefully hand-crafted image and perception. We want to have the proof that we are good people … because, "Look … here are all these other times we've gone so far out of my way for them."

There's a question on the quiz that you answered regarding paying the bill at the end of a group dinner. What did you choose? Your answer ties into your hidden agendas.

The Mouse will engage in a back and forth, pitiful exchange. "No, no, it's fine. I've got it. Are you sure? Are you sure though? But no, really, I can do it. But are you sure?" This has absolutely nothing to do with money and everything to do with a subconscious need to hear the other person say, "You don't owe me anything."

The Pitbull gets excited and almost competitive, then will let the other person pay but will slip a twenty into their purse, just to be able to put their head on the pillow that night with a "win."

The Phoenix will ensure that they win and pay the bill. Meanwhile everyone is made to feel awkward or downright unfuckingcomfortable.

Nobody actually wants someone to pay them back. They just want to make sure everyone knows the effort they put in. When you exist in this space, you constantly have your guard up. You constantly use your energy for manipulation, and you never spend any time with yourself. You fail to grow an identity.

Instead you have this cardboard version of yourself that everyone else sees. When that cutout gets called into question—you owe someone a favor, you show up late, you break something, you do something wrong—this endangers the cardboard façade. It triggers your survival and panic mode.

So something little, like another person trying to pay the bill, is a direct threat to your stability.

Now is the time to address your hidden agendas. Start out by recalling old events. Truly picture people's reactions, and with this new awareness, begin recognizing all the times you've made others uncomfortable. Vow to put an end to this cycle. And NOT because you are in any way responsible for the comfort of others, but because you owe it to yourself to exist in your true identity without the pressure to protect a cardboard cutout that honestly isn't even as cute as the real you anyway.

Releasing False Empathic Narratives

Not every Empath is a People Pleaser, but every People Pleaser is undeniably an Empath. And for Pleasers, rather than a gift to be respected, it's a skill honed and abused for the pure need to survive. When you strip down the ability for organic interaction, when you build up walls and have preconceived notions of what you want others to think about you, you then have to create a way to have an energetic exchange with others.

Unfortunately, People Pleasers use empathy as a scapegoat. "I feel their energy. I know what they are going through." Empathy allows us to think that we are psychic.

But for us? Empathy can be a goddamn liar.

If I see someone who is hurt and crying their eyes out, I can feel that same pain in their gut-wrenching sobs. I want to help, and much of that is true energetically. But so much is untrue. The tragedy is when a People Pleaser feels this energy, instead of accepting it for what it is, they try to heal it because it triggers their fear of the uncontrollable. If they can just make that person feel better, they themselves can get back to their comfort zone.

Because remember, for a People Pleaser to be okay, everyone else needs to feel okay. We take on the need to fix the situation and make it feel better. We take it on as if it's our own, and thus believe we have insight to the person and we are truly psychic for a moment.

The key we missed—the secret—is to let someone heal themselves. Respect their human experience. Trust them. Be there for them by simply listening without trying to fix anything. Let them respond as they want to. Let them ask for what they need instead of you guessing. Let them surprise you.

Releasing Manufactured Responsibilities

People Pleasers put a vast amount of responsibility on themselves. We make energetic agreements with other people. We make promises in friendships. We make agreements in business transactions. And then, of course, we overcommit and overthink all of them.

Agreements are the canvas for our integrity. There's something that happens to our energy when we constantly feel like we are confused, running late, forgetting something, etc.

You don't want to feel that way. You don't want to live life this way. But what can you do?

Possibly one of the most earth-shattering systems for managing this energetic battle was passed down from a past business mentor of mine, Matthew Cooke. Prepare to be just as annoyed at its perfect simplicity as I was ...

There are three things you can do with an agreement:

1. Uphold it.
2. Break it.
3. Renegotiate it.

... wait, what? There's a *third* option?! *punches hole in wall*

RENEGOTIATE?! Why have I never thought of that?

You mean we don't have to either kill ourselves to come through on our promise or forever flagellate ourselves for not measuring up?

Yup! So simple, right? You actually have the authority, as a human being who respects your own energy, to renegotiate your agreements. And guess what? People will appreciate this! They won't get mad at you. They get pissed when you break an agreement, not when you renegotiate. This lesson infuriated me to learn—far more than others in the group I was learning with. And it was because it spoke to a deeper level of how I needed to acknowledge the FAKE tasks I had always adopted for myself. So while others were making lists of their actual responsibilities and deciding what to do with them ... I was waking up to all of the lies I had tucked myself into a suffocating bed with. All the faux responsibilities I had tied to my ankles like cement. The majority of which no one had even, actually asked of me.

So it's time to start assessing those responsibilities. Each time you feel you need to do something, stop and ask yourself if that's true. If you don't stay at the office late today, then nobody else will do the work. Is that true? Or are you manufacturing responsibility? Are you keeping an agreement open because you want the emotional pay-off if you actually manage to complete it?

Pick something. Right now. Something that makes you anxious to think about completing. Or something you maybe wish you hadn't said yes to, but you were two drinks in at that party and were caught off guard by your mother-in-law. Or maybe even something you had to take on because someone else is a fuck-up. Don't worry ... you don't need to take action on it:

Current Manufactured Responsibility:

```



```

Now get real...

- Are you holding on for the emotional pay-out?
- Are you holding on strictly out of your lack of faith in the capability of others to complete it?
- Are you afraid to offend, hurt, or straight-up piss some people off?

Now imagine if, for just a moment, you, your energy, your happiness, your ease, and your comfort actually mattered. Would you rather set down this responsibility and walk away? That could look like a simple, "I'm sorry but I'm no longer in a position to complete this task for you, thank you for understanding." Or would you rather renegotiate it? (Pssst ... that usually looks like asking for help! I know, gasp!)

"A masterful romance of control for the ages"

This is all you need to get a fresh take on the "responsibilities" you're drowning in and then find graceful ways to reclaim your time and energy! My favorite thing to do is keep a "Faux Responsibilities" note open in my phone and write down every single thing that feels like a commitment but that I'm not 100 percent horny for. Then as I find the time, I pick one, do the above exercise, and immediately act on it. Take this process for a spin! It sure beats drowning.

This is your time to play the delegate. In a perfect world, who else can take care of some of the responsibilities in your life?

Releasing Toxic Control Patterns

You've released your narratives and responsibilities. Now it's time to recognize the ways you are a caretaker in your relationships—especially the times you emasculate, infantilize, and deprecate your loved ones.

Nobody wants to fuck their mom. *OK ... some people do but that's an entirely different self-help book ...*

You don't need to take care of your loved ones. Masculine individuals aren't boys who want a partner to look after them. Sure, they may love being taken care of. Who the hell doesn't?! But if you take care of every conversation, coach them through every argument, and premeditate every discussion—you'll slowly but surely strip away the sexy, innate ability they have and WANT to exercise in showing up to the partnership.

Feminine individuals aren't damsels who need saving. Sure a powerplay is hot AF in the sack, but don't infantilize them to secure your status as the hero. Their sexiest, most aligned power is not cultivated in simply being doted upon.

This holds true for your friends, your children, your parents, and your coworkers. Some people do this because they are control freaks. People Pleasers do it for survival. It's simply another technique to secure our addiction.

You purposefully emotionally cripple people, slowly, silently, so they will still need you. Meanwhile you feel worn out, exhausted, unsupported, and alone, because nothing would make you happier than to see everyone you love step out into the world filled with self-love and self-sufficiency ... well almost nothing ... because for now nothing feels as good as the manufactured dopamine of feeling needed.

It's like a parasite that makes sure someone out there needs you always, to perpetuate the idea that you're the only one who can give that much needed nourishment.

Instead you are robbing them of the ability to show up for themselves and to love you fully and organically. All because you don't believe a love that deep exists for you too.

I promise that it does. And you don't even have to believe me yet. Just start by considering this:

This person you've carefully curated and presented to the world, this identity you feel a stranger to, and more times than not feel utterly repulsed by, this People Pleasing you ... maybe they have all the love they deserve already. They've created the culture and the shockingly low standard of reciprocity all around them. The Pleaser in you has the love it deserves, because the Pleaser is merely a gardener. With plants they can keep at arm's reach, flowers that will never hold them, and a never-ending regimen of dependency. A masterful romance of control for the ages.

But that. Is. Not. You.

The love that exists for you is as deep as you are willing to love yourself. You're already a master at cultivating a beautiful garden. Now imagine a world where YOU get to be toes deep in the soil with all of the beautiful things and people you've grown to support your life. Because you are nourished from the same love you pour out to the rest of the garden.

That is you.

CHAPTER FOUR

OWN THE
WAGON

*Your independence should
never stand on the shoulders
of another's dependence*

IT'S TIME TO OWN your wagon and learn to start caring for yourself.

True love is a brick wall and doesn't require your barbed wire. You can enforce boundaries with love for yourself rather than aggression toward others. You don't have to have an "I don't give a fuck attitude" to put yourself first.

You shouldn't aspire to that at all ... because if you're being honest with yourself, weren't you kind of being a jerk before by being manipulative and not letting people own their own shit? You have the capacity to love so VERY deeply, and now it's time to find a way to give all that love in only the healthiest of ways!

Many People Pleasers at this stage start to push down their gift of loving. Don't do that. Don't half-ass love, dude. It will only negatively affect every single part of your life. The love you project results in the type of people you attract and the quality of love they can give you in return.

Sherie Goes to Prison

She'd gone to therapy. She'd done the relation-ship counseling. She learned all the names for her husband's moods and the rationale for her reactions to them. Some days she had the energy to coach him through his tantrums, some days she couldn't face his stonewalling.

Sherie was a teacher by profession and at heart and lived in a classroom of her own making, and she was content with that. It gave her joy to watch her patience and empathy transcribed into a lesson well absorbed and the smile on a gently enlight-ened face.

When her heart would break, be it because of a side-eye or a scoff under her husband's breath, she would identify WHY he was behaving that way, make peace with the inherent excuse therein, and hold the decision solely in her hands. But what Sherie didn't know was, if you've silenced your inner child and smothered your passion pulls and your soul's needs ... you actually lack the required information to make an educated decision.

In Sherie's mind there were two options:

1. Suck up her own reaction, try to connect with her husband, and try to coach him through the issue at hand.
2. Accept that she lacked the energy to take him on, and retreat to the spare bedroom to cry.

Eventually the spare bedroom became the only option. Day in and day out, Sherie would lock herself in, cry it out, and return to life on the other side of that door.

But what kind of life is that? Eventually those days became filled with anxiety, self-doubt, numbness, and dread. She lived this way for a while— half in the numb vacuum of forcing a smile, and half in the prison of her spare bedroom.

It took Sherie almost a year after her initial recovery began to let go of the manufactured responsibility of coaching her lover through their relationship and finally start hearing those passion pulls again. But she did it.

Without making him the bad man, without wearing the label of the woman who gave up, Sherie realized she didn't need to convict someone else to free herself from her own prison.

Honoring the Human

Many clients think that the solution to their behavioral addiction is to look into their friends' eyes, try to imagine what they are going through, and put themselves in their shoes.

No. People Pleasers aren't going to recover by constantly putting other people's shit on their plate and making their reactions about those around them. You need to focus on honoring humans, and that starts with honoring yourself.

Think about the things you want people to do for you. Think about the ways you want people to show up for you and respect you. Think about the ways you want people to honor your decisions, and communicate clearly. Know that you deserve this because you are just a force of nature, existing in a beautiful human body, doing the absolute best you can as you try to find all the joy awaiting you in this world.

Yes, you have decisions to make, but know that the choices you make for yourself in every single moment are truly for your best interest.

"You don't have to respect the PERSON to respect the human"

Even a negative choice doesn't mean you're a bad person. Choosing not to do the dishes because you're exhausted is self-care.

Breaking Down the Value System

It's time to tackle your faux-value system so you can begin to see all other humans in the exact same way. Don't take on their shit, don't try to fix their shit, and don't pity them. There's nothing worse than someone who's suddenly woke gaining their power from pitying everyone around them.

Nobody is better than you. Nobody is worse than you.

You're going to feel stupid at times. You're going to feel like a little kid at times. You're going to get triggered. Your addiction will be tested. But the difference between feeling like you've been punched in the gut and realizing you have something to learn is the value system you have in place. If you put others on a pedestal, you feel beneath them. If you put yourself on a pedestal, you think you know what's best, you know what they need, and you know how to take care of them better than they do.

Age, sex, lineage, race, success, experience, education, money ... NONE of this makes anyone a BETTER HUMAN than YOU.

It also doesn't make you better than someone else. It doesn't matter how connected you are to your empathy, it doesn't matter how much you've experienced, it doesn't matter how much you've lost … you're not better than another human.

When you believe, for even a moment, that whatever outcome you have deemed "best" is the end-all be-all, you're claiming god status. But, bitch, if you're a god, why you got so many problems? Step off and give yourself the peace and grace of knowing you are living your human experience in this one life to the best of the culmination of your experiences thus far.

Then take another step back and recognize that every other person in your life is existing in the same reality. Forgiveness, respect, acknowledgment, love, indifference, release … none of those require your judgment—so avoid that shit like the plague. You don't have to respect the PERSON to respect the human, and respecting the human is where our grace and sovereignty truly begin.

Many of us hold the value system as a security blanket, especially when going through a process like this where we are shedding old beliefs, shedding old people, and changing up the dynamic between the true us and the lucky humans who get to stay in our lives forever. As everything is shaking up, the value system is a comfortable thing to hold fast to. You're going against validation seeking, and you're learning to stand your ground. This timeframe is scary and tests old trauma patterns, and often the value system is the only thing you feel you can hang onto.

The key is to make your recovery about you. Many people climb that pedestal and feel their recovery is more important than their relationships. Their happiness is the only thing that matters. And while there is a gorgeous truth in that, it also causes a separation. The people in your life don't need a villain mask in order for you to do what's best for you and for you to find happiness. And more often than not, throwing out the baby with the bathwater is a lazy emotional bypass to taking back your power and responsibility in this life.

Frankly Just Aligning

The gun shaking in his hands, Frank screamed for the last time, "PLEASE DON'T GO! I'M NOT GONNA FUCKING MAKE IT WITHOUT YOU!" as she walked out the door.

They are both alive and well today, living separate lives. You, the reader, don't actually need to know any more detail than that. You don't need to know the play by play, how they got there, or any preface at all to this toxic point in their relationship. How they survived that intense evening ISN'T the power in this story. Because the culmination of this 15-year relationship is not written in their survival, it's written in their healing.

So let's begin there...

That night will be recounted to anyone willing to hold the space for it. It would be told in two very different versions. Both relive the terror, the sadness, and the hopelessness. Both declare emphatically their rightful position of victim that fueled their actions. Both recall feeling used up, spit out, and washed away. But only one will yearn for "closure."

The one with the loaded gun. The People Pleasing Addict. Frank.

He's the one who needs to hear some sort of validation for getting the help he needed. He's the one who just wants a window of communication to apologize, to have a real discussion, and to hear that she is doing the work to heal herself as well. He's the one who wants to clear the air of misconceptions, the one who needs to hear her say he's not a terrible human, and the one who wants acknowledgment of the love they shared at one point, surely, in all their time together. He's the one who wants to move on as something other than a lost cause in this world.

Several attempts later, through calls, texts, and a carefully curated letter to create a sense of closure for himself, all Frank received in return was a sense of confirmation that she was in fact telling a completely different story. A nightmare. And he was the monster in pursuit.

Gaslighting Yourself

You may be thinking this is about to be a breakup checklist of things to avoid so you're never confronted with your ex-lover's conflicting story of your experience with them ...

- Sever contact.
- Get all new friends.
- Burn their stuff.
- Fill the urge to creep their social media with cigarettes and casual sex.

But by now you know me better than that and are instead preparing yourself for an uncomfortable truth bomb ...

And I love you too much to disappoint you, so here ya go!

People Pleasing Addicts confuse "closure" with "aligned stories."

It's a survival mechanism that we need our version of what happened to line up with, and be mutually agreed upon by, the other party. It's designed to support the part of our addiction that wants to control the uncontrollable. The part that needs to be validated as a loving, caring, responsible human even when the relationship, friendship, or partnership is over.

It doesn't matter who ended it, or why. The Story rules us.

And when the stories don't line up? We'll use the other party's version of the story to gaslight ourselves.

Gaslighting: A specific form of psychological manipulation triggering doubt in the victim's memory of events, perceptions of reality, intuition, trust, and sense of self. The manipulator may be an exterior source, or internal dialogue induced by a trauma response. (What the fuck, right?)

Because their story IMPLIES something about us that denies the foundation of OUR story ...

Maybe they're feeling like the victim, when you know better.

Maybe they're feeling blindsided, when you were a clear communicator.

Maybe they're feeling betrayed, when your intentions were never questioned.

... their story, if true, would make yours untrue.

This sends us spiraling.

Existing in a world where we can't control someone's outward projection of us is a huge threat to our nervous system and kicks in our trauma responses. So we begin the diligent task of seeking the validation we think we need to feel safe again. We try to control the uncontrollable, without stopping to consider the impossibility of our search. I mean, shit, what's more uncontrollable than someone else's trauma response? (And the end of a relationship is traumatic. Period. It creates its own little set of trigger patterns that, if you're not careful, will carry into your next relationship. So no matter the lack of validity you feel in their version of the story, you can't deny them this trauma.)

And for a Pleaser, when we are faced with something we CANNOT control, it's an alarm screaming, "WE ARE NOT SAFE!" Whatever spiraling out of control looks like for you, buckle up 'cause that's where you're headed. We become obsessed with the idea of closure.

Gut Check: CLOSURE FOR A PLEASER IS NOTHING MORE THAN THE IDEA THAT WE CAN FORCE SOMEONE TO VALIDATE OUR EXPERIENCE.

But no matter how hard you try, you're left feeling unsupported in what deep down you know is reality. Refer again to the above gaslighting realness.

Me: *mic drop*

Literally every client of mine: "OK ... well fuck. Are you gonna tell me how NOT to do that then?"

Me: "OH! Haha ... yeah totally! I've already told you! RESPECT THE HUMAN!"

Them: *face palm* "ughh ... of course ... you know how annoying you are when I don't want to deal with my own shit, don't you?"

Me: *shimmies obnoxiously*

You don't have to agree with or respect the person to look beyond their skin and see the humanity beneath. This humanity would tell you that EVERYONE has trauma responses. Everyone. And this human's survival mechanism to survive the relationship's end is as justified and important as yours—even if their story doesn't align with yours.

At this point you might be thinking, "Coooool. Cool. Cool. Cool ... so I'm just supposed to sit back and agree or feel crazy?!"

Nope! I invite you instead to repeat this:

"I will live out my story. They will live out their story. Our stories are no longer intertwined. Their story has nothing to do with me. Mine has nothing to do with them. And we are both forever free to rewrite them as we heal from our own traumas."

Armed with this mantra, Frank no longer requires validation for his story to feel true and safe in his own system. What's more, he can finally release the impulse to shatter her story as a means to recover his own sense of safety.

I invite you to make a list of the encounters in your life for which you still desire closure. And really ask yourself if that desire is just a clever disguise for "Aligned Story Seeking" for validation, or if instead there is a means within your own body to regain your safety and sense of self.

Accept and Respect

And now for a bit more on the topic of respecting other humans and how it pertains to situations outside of Aligned Story Seeking.

Does this mean you need to forgive everyone? Fuck no. Do you need to find a common ground with them? Fuck no.

But can you find ways to deal with your own trauma AND still respect the human in front of you? Fuck YES!

If you can accept the things you've done—the manipulation, the ickiness—as not who YOU really are, then you have to accept that other people have done things that don't make them who they are.

They are human beings, with inner children who are desperate to be heard, living life the best they can with the resources they've gathered thus far.

You can love someone, you can release someone, and you can forgive someone without it being tied to judgment or having anything to do with the person they currently are.

I named my program People Pleasers Autonomous because my main goal has always been to get clients back to autonomy. It's not just about discovering your true identity, it's about discovering your entire nation you've abandoned up to this point. Nobody has been manning the gate or making sure people are fed, because you've been using your resources for everyone else. You have to reclaim your own sovereignty and gain a sense of autonomy. The easiest and fastest way to do that is to honor other humans. Look someone in the eye, drop back into your center, your own autonomy, and release the other bullshit. I know an even playing field feels like completely uneven terrain for a Pleaser at first, but it's the only path to your autonomy.

Refuse to Clap Back

Energy can be distributed—much like a battery—in a positive and negative manner. When you're on high alert, constantly looking to defend your ground, you are battle ready with a negative energy churning inside you. Your subconscious stands in the soldier position, waiting and waiting, until it bubbles to the surface when you least expect it. You are ready to change people's minds or make them realize that it's not worth arguing with you because you are so above that shit.

Even if you don't feel angry, there is negative energy in what you may be confusing for empowerment. It's a ticking time bomb that you planted on your own turf, and it's prepped and waiting for some unrelated trigger to set it the fuck off. Have you ever had a moment in time where you exploded, absolutely lost your shit, and had no idea where it came from? Or spiraled negatively but didn't know why? It's because you've been holding that negative energy, and it's time to get it under control so you don't make a habit of reacting poorly to the ones who are starting to love the real you.

Stop wearing your confidence as a costume. When you're secure and living in a place of love and abundance, you don't clap back at people. You don't get shittily defensive.

Let's pretend you are on a health and fitness journey, pairing it with your PPA Recovery. When you're out to dinner with a group of friends and someone comments on why you only ordered a salad—you realize they may have something internally to work on, but you don't react. You don't explode. You take a breath, know it has nothing to do with you, speak from a place of calm, and say from your heart with a smile on your face. "I'm not feeling like fried chicken, it doesn't sound great for my body right now. But I'm glad you're giving your body what it wants and I'm excited to watch you enjoy it!"

Whereas, if you were still holding strong to your addiction you might respond from a spicy place of, "You do you. You can poison your body, but I'm not going to." This is actually your own defense mechanism. It's unnecessary, and you're never going to get a friend to join you on a health quest by being on the attack!

You will never get empowerment by standing on the shoulders of someone who is not empowered. You will never feel better by telling your friends why you're better than they are. You will never move forward with your behavioral addiction by clapping back.

Catty ain't cute. It's deflective and skeevy.

Don't be skeevy.

Navigate Conflict, Don't Avoid It

We've talked about it before. Don't avoid conflict. Don't manipulate the outcomes. You're not psychic. Life is an adventure, and adventures are meant to surprise you. Sure, it's uncomfortable and scary. But it's time to navigate conflict by speaking your truth while honoring another human's right to do with it what they will.

When you pre-manipulate a conversation, you will always be disappointed. It will never go exactly as planned, and you'll be left feeling railroaded. Even if you say exactly what you want to say, if the other person doesn't offer a reflection that makes you feel seen, understood, and heard, you come out of it exhausted and wondering what happened. You're robbing those around you and stripping away their ability to even hear what you're trying to really say.

The success of communication is not measured by the outcome.

It's measured by your truth being spoken at all costs.

(Wanna know the real reason why you think you're psychic? Because no matter the angle of someone's mental picture of you, EVERY human paints a bit of a self-portrait. Womp womp. It's easy to truly think you know someone when you aren't differentiating their beauty from your own.)

Respect humans in the way you want to be respected.

Communication: Listening and Being Heard

When it comes to communication, it's time to listen and be heard. That does not mean you should mirror! I know ... I know. Mirroring is a popular technique you may have already learned from your psychotherapist. But it doesn't work for a Pleaser! It's impossible to be present for someone else and listen intentionally while keeping a mental placeholder for your opposing view. The urge to keep a pin in what you want to say while the other person talks is the fear that the narrative will unravel if you forget your talking points or let your position slip.

Perspective shifts can't take hold in that environment. For either of you. And to denounce the possibility that YOUR perspective is the one that needs shifting is to take a seat at the top of your faux-value system ... and that's just a big fat sack of EW.

We are master jugglers of duality and often wait for our turn to speak. But mirroring is for people who aren't drowning in the need for validation or the need to manipulate and control the situation. We can mirror just fine. We can mirror like a pro. But the goal here is organic communication and to remain present in the moment. By mirroring, you're actually trying to remember what the other person said so you can prove you were listening. You get lost in your own script of your own retelling and don't hear what's actually being said. This can be creepy and manipulative in its own right, causing the conversation to run in circles because nobody is listening.

That is not communication!

Dedicate your ears to truly hearing humans; believe it or not ... it will only help you be heard.

A note on politics ... most People Pleasers hate to engage in political conversations. Whether you're the Pitbull and don't want to feel uneducated, the Phoenix whose hackles are already raised to defend their stance, or the Mouse who feels nobody will listen to them anyway, it's okay. This is one topic where I encourage People Pleasers to stay silent if they are still working on their addiction. These conversations can be a trigger in a time of healing. Not engaging doesn't mean you are uneducated. It doesn't make you less of an adult. It just means you have a behavioral addiction that knows when validation is on the line, your throat is going to close up.

That's not to say you shouldn't be political. It's now more important than ever to find your autonomy, find what you believe in, and ACT ON IT. Don't vote for a candidate or measure just because your significant other is. Rather, sit and figure out your identity. Research and decide for yourself. Autonomous politics and activism can look like you NOT starting an argument. It can look like you researching, voting, and doing what makes YOU feel good without seeking any outside validation for it.

A Present Presence

You exist in the now, not the future or the past. People Pleasers have a tendency to use past occurrences or future possibilities to impact their present. Perhaps you're a babe in a club, trying to look sexy. You suddenly have a fear that some cute hottie is going to walk in and see your stomach sticking out, so you suck in your gut all night. That quick blip caused you to jump into the future, determine the worst possible outcome, come back to the now, and try to fix something to keep it from happening. It's a need to control the uncontrollable, so you attempt to predict all the bad outcomes and negate them.

Other times you jump back in reflection. You're laughing with your friends, and suddenly you remember the fury in Jon's eyes when your cackles kept him from sleeping. You correct your volume in the hopes that nobody calls you out.

Your "path" doesn't matter. Anything you've done or achieved in the past doesn't exist in the future. You can't do anything to change the past. You achieved it, it existed, and you've moved forward. Trophies don't guarantee you happiness or clarity ... nor does your projected future. You can have a lovely, amazing existence with the most beautiful future in your mind ... and do one tiny thing today to fuck it all up.

You exist in THIS moment. Anything that happened in the past—as horrible or embarrassing as it was—didn't kill you. You are you, sitting here in this moment now.

So when you find your mind starting to wander to the past or future—as it will—repeat to yourself the following:

I exist now. I exist now. I exist now.

Know that you're in this body, in this chair, in this exact moment. You are a human and not a psychic. You can't know what someone is about to tell you. You don't know how they feel. Every time you start to manipulate or project—or you realize that you're not listening to your partner—pull yourself back to the present. Repeating the mantra takes up much less space cognitively than quizzing yourself on what they're telling you. It allows you to sit, be present, and give yourself the freedom to respond organically.

And if you find yourself reacting to the conversation, getting angry at the other person, and pulling them into your bullshit value system, take a moment to change the mantra to:

WE exist now.

You are two humans, sitting there, and nothing is going to come of the interaction if you bring the past and the future into it. You both just have to be here, in the present.

Looking for the Easter Eggs

Now is the time to develop a sense of intrigue for surprises and mishaps. Look for Easter eggs instead of landmines.

My mother, a self-proclaimed self-sufficient woman, recently visited me with my nephew. On the day she was supposed to drive home, she hopped into her truck and it wouldn't start. It had been making strange noises throughout the day, and she would make some dramatic comment but not look into it. I had opted to distance myself from her foreboding energy because it was her vehicle, and if she didn't want to take it in to get looked at … well, that was on her.

With my mom being a Phoenix, I knew that if I offered her advice she'd reject it anyway! We've had those back-and-forth conversations of her complaining, me suggesting something, and her arguing the point. So that day I didn't engage. Until I had no choice.

The truck wouldn't start, and she turned to me and said, "I told you something was wrong with my truck!"

I returned the look and said, "No. You mentioned there was a noise, and then you chose not to do something about it. This isn't because of me. I didn't convince you of anything. Take a deep breath and let's figure this out."

She got massively offended and started to panic. She started crying and said, "This has never happened to me."

I was so confused. "Your car breaking down? Yes it has." I thought maybe her memory had failed again, because her car had broken down in the past. I was with her when it happened.

She shook her head. "You don't understand. I've never been ALONE when my car is broken down."

My nephew chimed in with a confused, "But Ahdri and I are here."

And then I got it. At that moment in time my mother didn't have a man in her life to help her with this. Her boyfriend had just left her, and she has rarely been single in her entire life. So, this was a very raw, very real feeling of helplessness, and she began to spiral. "I don't have the money for this. I don't even know what to do. Do I need a tow truck? How am I going to get home today?"

Rather than get frustrated, I tried my best to calm her with the truth. "One. You're safe. Two. I live here, you have a bed to sleep in. Three. We've got our phones; we will figure this out."

I realized in that moment we were both putting in equal amounts of energy for different things. She was spiraling and finding the doomsday scenario in the present, and I was searching for the Easter egg. She was only delayed four hours after we called the mechanic and he came out and fixed the truck. If she had left earlier, she might have broken down on the side of the road, or in the middle of the night, or she could have even gotten into an accident. SO many worse things could have happened but were avoided.

If you search for Easter eggs, you're searching for solutions. If you search for catastrophes, you're just setting yourself up for more catastrophes. It's not about sunshine and roses all the time. You can give yourself the space to be mad and annoyed, confused and embarrassed, but do that shit WHILE you hunt for Easter eggs.

Working with Your Triggers

You're about to exist on a new vibration, and you can't take people with you. If they're meant to meet you there, their own vibrations will shift, but you can't do it for them. The key is to know the nonsense that used to exacerbate your condition and be able to hold your clarity in those moments.

Recognize the feelings you get when you start to get triggered. It might be tension in your chest, or you may find yourself clenching your jaw. These physical triggers are clues that you're uncomfortable. Start to recognize them—either in the moment or later in the day when you reflect—and then name them.

Oh. My chest feels tight. I'm clenching my fists.

By recognizing them and naming them, you start to carve out new neuro patterns to replace your trigger responses. I laugh when I fall because it's a trigger response I've created. My sister gets tears in her eyes, because that's a hold-over from her youth when my mother would respond fiercely from her own fear with a sharp and reprimanding, "You're fine! Shake it off!"

Every trigger response can be adjusted.

Once you've recognized and named them, now it's time to ground your way through the triggers with the presence present.

You're not going to have a therapy session in that moment. All you're going to do is recognize the discomfort, sit in it, and wonder what it all might mean. Let's say you have to give a presentation at work. Suddenly your hands clench because you have anxiety. That's happening because you're projecting stage fright into the future. Bring it back to the present. Remind yourself, "I exist now. I exist now." Or repeat, "Respect the human." (Imagining the crowd in their underwear isn't necessary when you're envisioning them as capable, loving humans who reflect your love back to you.) Do whatever is necessary to bring you back down into the moment.

I realize it's hard. If you're someone obsessed with personal growth, it can be tempting to find the next breakthrough by diving in deep to see what each feeling and physical reaction means. You can do that AFTER you're grounded. Get yourself back into the present, do your mantra, and then you can evaluate your present state.

- Am I hungry?
- Am I hydrated?
- Have I exercised today?
- Did I get enough sleep?
- Do I need to start looking into therapy?
- Should I get a coach?
- Do I need a self-care day?
- When's the last time I got out of the house?

Get your body back on the same page, calm yourself, and then you can open up the space to react and respond organically as a human.

Falling off the Wagon

As you work through your triggers, you will keep falling off the wagon. It's okay, and it certainly isn't as devastating as you make it.

It took me over seven hours to complete a full marathon, not because of a torn IT band and a ruptured bursa, not because of the stress fractures in my left foot, but because I went the wrong way at the fork and followed the half marathoners for about a mile before I realized it and had to turn back.

The entire way back to the fork I was so damn mad. Suddenly the excitement and tenacity I had of, "Hell yeah, halfway mark, here I come," turned into, "Oh fuck.

I have to do this another 13 plus miles," and I started to cry while I was running.

If you're thinking crying and cardio don't mix, you're right! But, before I could completely hyperventilate, I found the fork and literally got back on track. You know what I thought then? "Last half, here I come, bitch." (And if you need a moment to repeat that in a Jesse Pinkman voice, I'll allow it...)

Here's the point. Recognizing you fell sucks, but not as badly as getting to the wrong finish line and never noticing. The moment you get back on track feels like you've been given this extra shot of "fuck yeah" in your joints. I bought myself a "27.1, I got lost" headband as a joke to help me remember the decision I made to get back at it, even though it meant more work. I later gave the headband to a motivational speaker as a memento after he told his own epic version of a similar face-palm marathon moment. And damn, if I'm not alone in that one-of-a-kind dumbassery, you'll never be alone in fall-ing off your recovery wagon!

Lazy Diagnosis

Don't confuse laziness with a lack of motivation.

Sometimes you might fall off the wagon and become unmotivated. You haven't showered. The house is a mess. You confuse it with depression or laziness. I hate the word lazy. Because once you say it out loud, it becomes this tangible diagnosis that can't be treated.

If you are lazy, YOU ARE LAZY. It's like saying, "I'm an asshole!" If that were true, there would be no changing it. But it being untrue only degrades all the true facets of current imbalance in your body that need your attention, and creates yet another erroneous layer to the false, self-deprecating identity you've been working so hard to shed.

Feelings of laziness can appear on any transformative journey. Health. Career. Mental wellness. Don't do it. Don't throw in the towel. Don't give yourself an incurable diagnosis.

When you do that, you remove all hope. Hope is the only thing that gives you excitement and energy to move forward.

You're not an asshole. You have no "inner saboteur." You are you. You are human.

You're simply not present! So pull yourself into the present, and see what it is you actually need to propel you to the next step.

The Reset Button

Starting over doesn't exist. It's not a thing that can happen. You're intelligent; you know you can't pause life. We spend so much time deciding if we can start over and how to do it. But the fact is, you screw up, you learn from it, and you move on. The experiences make up who you are!

You can't change the past, but that leads to a heaviness that many people can't climb out from under.

There's no pause and starting over, but there IS a reset button.

Find a visual spot on your body. For me, it's my nose. For some, it's their bellybutton. Some of my clients put their hand over their heart or groin. Some slap their own ass. Choose yours by picking a spot that connects your mind with your body and tells you you're okay. You are safe. You have infinite chances, until you die, to get this right. You're allowed to do it better this time. You don't have to pretend something didn't happen. You don't have to pretend you didn't screw up. You're allowed to move forward with or without apology. You get to have and do better in the future.

The reset button forces introspection in the moment. You can't reset a fight, but you can hit your reset button and tell the other person, "Look, I did not mean that. I have no idea where that came from. I'm so sorry I said that. Please accept my apology."

It's possible to be present with yourself and your loved ones and break the cycle! You won't be able to implement this overnight, but the more you practice, the easier and better it becomes. For now, just start to use the reset button when you begin to feel guilt, shame, and self-degradation.

The reset button allows you to stand in integrity with yourself. It allows you to promise you will do better because you deserve to have and feel the best this life has to offer. It allows you to take ownership of your worth and responsibility for your actions.

You get unlimited chances to stand in integrity with your words.

Try it out!

Harnessing the Gift of Empathy

So yeah … you actually DO have a gift. You have intuition. You have empathy. (But here's the thing. You're still not special. EVERYONE is special.)

You can, however, harness that gift. You are never closer to your alignment and energetic gift than when you are staring into the face of grief. And if you can harness it rather than drown in it, you can change the world.

People Pleasers can seem volatile and unpredictable to the people around them when they sit in their grief, because grief doesn't have time for bullshit.

Imagine your true alignment with yourself and your soul's purpose as a door. Sometimes you get so close to the door you can almost touch it. Those are the best and most fascinating times of your life. But you've never actually opened the door and walked through ... because that's unheard of.

When tragedy strikes and you're grieving for something, that door gets blown off the hinges—just for that period of time. You have no time for small talk or bullshit or wearing other people's emotions. You just have time to sit with your human body and reflect. You're in pain, and this is the time you see things a little more clearly. You hold the grief as your own emotion and take the time to sit with yourself.

That's the gift you need to harness and take forward with you. The ultimate gift of clarity. Otherwise, we drown in the blur.

Unconscious & Bleeding

Though I was only 16 years old, being homeschooled meant I was the primary filler for callouts and short staffing at the local McDonalds in Loganville, Georgia.

During what felt like a routine never-ending shift, I saw my assistant manager, James, a close friend at the time, and grown-ass man, basically lose his shit after a call he took in the back office.

"I thought he was on the East coast??" he had said before he slammed the phone down, crying, and fleeing out the back door.

I assumed it was about his son but would find out how incorrect that assumption was in about ten excruciatingly long minutes.

My shift manager, Sarah, approached me and asked for my headset. I got bitchy, as if my abilities as a drive-thru operator were in question. But I stopped when I saw the color drain from her already alabaster cheeks.

I recognized instantly the heaviness in the air and felt its direct, unwavering connection to me. In the moments before my mother walked through the door, all possible work-related obstacles having been strategically removed from her path by the staff, I felt it.

The unsolicited empathy. At 16, I didn't know what to do with it besides fight it. I was a Kent. It was MY job to help people through THEIR tragedies ... what was all this fuckery? Why were people looking at ME like that? Like they wanted to touch me and pull me close, but at the very same time distance themselves from the shrapnel I was bound to spray at any moment.

My mother approached the counter, and she looked so very sorry. But all I could feel was anger. I knew she wasn't going to speak, but I could see it in her eyes. My anger grew, and I shouted to anyone who would listen, "What the FUCK is going on?"

I knew not to ask, "Did I do something wrong?" or "Am I in danger?" or any other desperate version to clear the air of confusion.

In that moment, Katy, a dear friend and co-worker, emerged from the back and went straight to my mother in a panic, sobbing, "I heard too much, I'm sorry! I heard too much!"

Then I knew.

Not the devastating news itself, but that I needed to shut the fuck up and follow my mother to her silver Monte Carlo.

In one last act of defiance, while sitting on the hot black leather, I held the car door open and demanded she reveal the truth before I let her drive us away from that parking lot.

She took a deep breath and said the words I was silently begging her not to. "We lost your father."

There it was, like a slab of concrete reality hitting me in the face. My father was a long-haul truck driver, and suddenly James's seemingly innocent question from earlier made sense. He knew how close I was to my dad, so while the location didn't actually matter, it rattled the irrelevant line of questioning from him all the same. Actually …

irrelevant doesn't even begin to scrape the surface of all the questions you would think should have followed.

Because Dad wasn't on the East Coast—he wasn't even on the west coast—he was found in the Midwest, hung by a T-shirt in the cab of his truck.

I wouldn't find out these details for weeks, but it didn't matter. The impact was the same. Cold. Hard. Impossible. I couldn't breathe. I couldn't see.

I did in fact try to escape. I spilled out of the car onto my hands and knees. I beat the pavement, I heard my mother sob, and I heard her apologize over and over again. I felt Katy's arms around me, releasing her own sadness. Yet in that moment I had never felt more alone. I felt betrayed. My soul played tug-o-war with feeling everyone's emotions around me while resisting my own.

Then my mother's tears became piercingly clear. Like the only sound on earth. And in an instant, I went from feeling betrayed and alone to feeling like the biggest piece of shit on the planet. She had just lost the love of her life. She now had to watch her children suffer while knowing she couldn't take away their pain. I felt so bad. I didn't want to be the reason she hurt MORE. My breath began syncing with hers, my tone calmed to match hers, and we began the People Pleasing/Empath/Kent woman dance of simultaneously soothing each other. But my body knew better; this car ride would be nothing compared to the days, weeks, and life to come. I couldn't keep up the soothing game; it would all be too much, and I would need a way out.

So I made a quick, quiet decision. A choice that would protect those around me from any additional trauma I could bring them. It was only when I tasted blood that I realized I had begun biting my lip to keep from crying aloud. There I sat, head against the door, and as the blood pooled under my tongue in a slow trickle, I heard my own voice as if drowning from afar say, "They can't handle your pain too." I would wrap that toxic phrase around me like a warm blanket for 16 more years.

I'm only human and passed out from the pain of severing a dime-sized piece from the interior of my bottom lip. I don't recall what it felt like to pull up to our beautiful farm on that perfectly crisp April Fool's Day in 2001. I do remember when my Uncle Jason (not a real uncle, but a friend of my parents) plucked me from the front seat of the car. My mother told him I had passed out from exhaustion and asked if he could take me inside for a nap. I wanted so badly to clutch Jason's neck and sob ...

but more than anything I could feel the sigh of relief in everyone's imagining my much needed "nap." So I kept my eyes closed.

As Jason lowered me to the couch and looked at my mouth, he yelped when he saw the blood. My mother immediately answered, "She must have bit her lip on the ride home, trying not to cry."

I felt understood, and safe ... at least enough to pass out again for real.

At the wake, I would continue to battle with maintaining actual consciousness and pretending when it suited my energy levels. I began wondering if my body was in cahoots with my secret when, as I approached his casket, my knees buckled, my father's foreign, embalmed face rushed closer to mine, and the room went black.

There was a mutual understanding in that moment.

What I wouldn't realize for over a decade was that my mind and body had my back and con-stantly reinforced escape routes for me. A fear of freefalling protected me from success. An autoim-mune disease protected me from recognizing body and weight issues. An ITB injury protected me from running marathons ever again. An onslaught of ill-ness, locked chakras, and throat issues protected

me from a blossoming singing career. A heart condition protected me from conflict.

In a pile on the floor by my father's lifeless body,
I learned I could do ANYTHING I put my mind to.

Witness, Receive, or Be Burdened with Energetic Information

As you continue to harness your empath skills, it's
key to determine if you are feeling your own emotions
or piggybacking off someone else's. Falling into someone else's energetic information feels good. Yes it's painful to support someone in their grief, but it also feels
good to People Pleasers on a subconscious level. It's an
excuse to release your own pent-up emotions and adopt
someone else's tragedy as your own for a moment.

But come on now, while documenting a beautiful fire,
you wouldn't throw the camera in the flame for solidarity. Yet you do it with your body, your mental state, and
your emotions when you fall into someone else's energetic information. You have to learn how to see the information and choose whether to document it or simply be
a lens.

Here's the thing. You don't owe anyone anything.
You're not obligated to give your gift of empathy to anyone. Your gift is precious, but you're not the only one who
has it, and you're nobody's obligatory savior. Phoenixes

especially tend to dive into the active service role when tragedy strikes. Whenever there was a death, funeral, or tragedy, my mother would take us to that person's house so we could clean, cook their meals, or plan the funeral.

Unfortunately, those acts of service are a way of avoiding the difficulty and realness in witnessing and connecting with that person. This is when you need to ask, "What do you need?" Most people don't need someone to do laundry and cook meals. They need someone to sit with them and listen to what they actually need.

Even if you get good at witnessing rather than being burdened by energetic information, it's very common to believe that you're the only one who can connect with someone in that way and help them. You're not. You ARE special, but there are many incredible people who can connect with someone in the only way they can.

The following words around this can and should be applied when, at any point in your life, you find yourself saying, "I'm the only one they've ever opened up to like this" or "I understand them in a way no one else can" etc.

Never let your gift of love and empathy obligate you to another human.

Now, these words irritated an online follower recently, and he responded with a declarative comment about how much he loved his wife and would do anything for her.

He missed the point completely.

But TO his point, I still stand firm in that we should never feel obligated to the people we choose to love and support—such as our spouses or children. Obligation should never be what keeps you in any relationship. Obligation is devoid of choice. And if I told you I hadn't had clients who were being seriously, abusively taken advantage of by their spouses, and in some cases even their children ... I'd be full of shit.

So I'll repeat it.

Never let your gift of love and empathy obligate you to another human. It's a GIFT. It's yours to give, and it's yours to take away when it risks draining you.

Being Healthy in Giving Love

As we end this chapter and move to the next, I ask you to challenge the times you're feeling called to give love. Step back and ask yourself the following questions:

- Does this make me happy?
- Do I desire something in return?
- Am I getting it?

It's not fucked up to desire reciprocity. Your energy is an investment, and if you're dabbling in a bank outside your own body, you better be seeing a return. We are taught as Pleasers that it's okay that we don't get the same love that we put out.

IT'S NOT FUCKING OKAY.

Having said that, I'd love to reiterate the difference between rationing your giving only to get, and giving to yourself so openly and prolifically that you naturally attract reciprocity.

CHAPTER FIVE

PERMISSION
GRANTED

*Passion NEEDS your Attention, Intensity,
and Action ... NOT your Commitment.
Don't be afraid of change; it's where the
next amazing adventure awaits.*

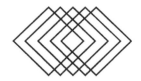

IT'S TIME TO CULTIVATE only healthy relationships.

You don't have to be Edward Scissorhands and cut away all your current connections. When you live in integrity with yourself, the incompatible ones will unwind and fall away on their own. Showing up for yourself in every relationship in your life allows every other human the freedom to act organically and truly decide what they are willing to show up for.

A LOT of the people you've been picking up the slack for would have fallen off your radar a long time ago had you not kept dragging them along. And it's not simply that you made it easy for people to love you; it's deeper and grosser. You actually made up their minds for them ... to love you. Blarf.

Who Are You Really?

You have true, beautiful parts of yourself, and you need to start embracing them.

Yes, your inner child was acting out all this time, but that was only because it needed to be validated and loved. You have so much love to give both your inner child AND others. Your gifts allow you to be creative, compassionate, and offer love hand-tailored to each individual. This can be very meaningful, and you don't want to push that part away.

The manipulative person that came through your addiction is NOT WHO YOU ARE.

So who are you?

You get to figure it out!

People Pleasing Addicts, upon "waking up" to their addiction, find themselves devoid of identity. They've been wearing their empathy as a disguise, as it allows

"be exponentially more profound than some soulmate, twin flame bullshit"

them to keep afloat when drowning in the identities of the ones they love.

What do you want?

If that question is confronting, you're not alone. It's supposed to be. It has to be. And you need to feel the discomfort and endlessly terrifying possibility of it and all its implications.

When we find ourselves emotionally alone (which most Pleasers do anything in their power to avoid, thus the only reason we would find ourselves emotionally abandoned is if someone is upset with us), the ocean of disappointment we've created in someone else is all we know how to feel. But as you wake up and move toward recovery, you will recognize the shift from taking on everyone else's emotions to discovering who YOU really are.

You no longer have to tailor yourself. You no longer have to live in a constant state of social anxiety. The fears that have controlled you daily no longer can.

My Favorite Color: A Rainbow

"I've lost myself. All I know is that I'm a mom, or a wife, or a nurse … I don't know who I am or what I want … I don't even know what my favorite color is!"

These are words my clients say. I wish I could say they were rare, but they aren't.

Not knowing your favorite color because of the empathic disguises you've worn for everyone else all these years hardly seems enough to denote an identity crisis. But the roots of this tiny implication sink deep into every decision you've ever made.

Picture this:

You're a woman six years into a committed relationship with the most perfect, strong, loving, funny, sexy, compassionate man on the planet. You've found it. It's yours. Your soulmate.

Until something changes. A miniscule shift. You didn't see it, hear it, or feel it. The only evidence that it even occurred is an unrecognizable heaviness. A feeling that something is about to break, a building anxiety, a sadness ... a rapidly gaining monster without a face.

Your sex begins to suffer inexplicably.

You seek out every option, therapy, method, strategy, healing, and help you can find. But nothing mends the shift. In a cruel way, every attempt to heal it only cracks it further open. And knowing the future of your life exists in the unknown depths of the cavern below ... your desperation grows ...

Goosebumps no longer erupt when he whispers in your ear.

Wet no longer flows when he tangles his fingers fiercely in your hair.

Even self-pleasure is flooded with the same numbing gray, like a punishment for existing at all.

"Maybe it's the medication I'm on." ... Discontinue medication.

The monster still gains.

"Maybe it's my body." ... Lose 40 pounds and become the healthiest external version of yourself yet.

Even closer it gains ...

"Maybe it's my environment." ... Sell everything, travel the country.

The monster's breath is so hot on your neck now ...

Three years into this exhausting hunt, your perfect man walks into the bathroom at 4:00 a.m. to find you with a pocketknife half an inch deep into your skin in a desperate attempt to remove the birth control implant because ...

"It's the one thing I haven't tried."

The finger pointing never seems to end, and they all point at you with no relief.

Every step closer to discovering why you're so "broken" only breaks you more. As if you're so off the mark that you're getting punished for every step further in the wrong direction.

Until the day comes as you watch your 11th anniversary approach ... the 5th anniversary of your brokenness ...and you have to tell him the ONE thing you have never tried. The ONE thing you've NEVER allowed yourself to see.

And why would you?

You had a perfect life, a perfect man, a perfect business, a perfect family, a perfect home...

But perfect isn't an indicator of your PPA recovery.

Perfect isn't a barometer of your truth.

Creating perfection in everyone and everything around you never results in your beautiful self-portrait. Rather the sacrifice and the silence it took to achieve that false reality will be the subject. The empty eyes. The sunken chest where your fulfilled heart should have been.

You see it, you can't unsee it, the ONE THING that you've denied yourself to exist in your happiest life.

And with six little words ... you willingly shatter your entire perfect existence.

Because you, a recovering Pleasing Addict, knows it's the only way to your truth.

The monster sinks its fangs in as if to say... If YOU don't say it, I will.

So you take a deep breath and say them:

"I think I might be Gay."

... and fall into the caverns below.

It was October 2019 when those words slid from my gums.

Another two and a half months of compromise and discovery were to follow, until the day it was no longer a question. 1/2/2020. I remember the night vividly ... I knew the next morning would be the end of us. There would be no more "working through it" or "figuring it out."

Sure enough, Derren stood at the foot of the bed with tears in his eyes. He knew the energy had shifted and he said, "Just tell me, tell me what you finally know."

"I'm Gay."

Then as the cruelest juxtaposition, I watched the man I'd tenderly cared for over the past 11 years crumble ... while the monster released its grip from my throat, sank back into my body, and gave me the warmest hug.

Not knowing your favorite color is a tip of the iceberg of this addiction. Self-sacrifice is a monster we create. Your identity IS, in fact, EVERYTHING.

So let's start small and uncover what your favorite color truly is.

Mine is a rainbow.

Taking Back Your Power

That narcissistic relationship or emotionally abusive friendship you are/were in? You made that possible by showing up for THEM rather than yourself. When an encroachment on your boundaries is detected and not shut down, you are choosing the role of victim. Showing up for yourself takes back your power.

Simply put, if you had a chronically late employee, would you make it your job to show up at their home, bathe them, dress them, and drive them to work to ensure they were on time? The answer to that, especially at this point in the book, should be a resounding FUCK NO.

And it doesn't have to seem so harsh. Life isn't about letting the weak ones drown (which is what it can feel like when a Pleaser practices showing up for only themselves at first), but it IS about taking your controlling grip off the path other humans may be destined for. Maybe working for you isn't how that human would thrive in their life. Maybe dating you isn't what's truly best for your lover. Maybe knowing you isn't what will change your friend's life.

One of the saddest things I've read online, in the wake of our emotionally bypassing "woke" culture, was this statement:

"Never forget: You were put on this earth to make someone's life better, and someone was put here to make your life better too."

I detest half-truths. Which makes me a very talkative person because I believe most concepts and anecdotes deserve to be expounded upon before they're taken at flaccid face value.

No matter your religion or ideology, you are on this planet to live an entire human rotation of life. You weren't placed here to make a difference or save anyone. If you devote your time here to healing and accessing the truest, most love-fueled parts of your gifts, the impact will be exponentially more profound than some soulmate, twin flame bullshit.

It's that type of point-blank, self-sacrificing for the "bigger picture" nonsense that is deepening the hole in this rapidly growing martyrdom culture. And it's the exact jumping-off point for every relationship, friendship, or partnership you pulled out of your ass and forced down the throat of those you decided you were here to fix.

The reality is that for every person who would be better off NOT being dragged around by your vigilance, there is another who can show up, meet you, see you, hear you, understand you, and nourish you. And they won't require your energy be poured into them. They will be attracted by the resonance of your energy as it's poured over and over back into yourself.

And THIS is why you don't need to put the burden on yourself of determining who to keep and who to cut away.

Imagine you invited a group of people to climb a mountain with you. As you start, some of them turn back to go home. Some stop halfway up the mountain. Some get close to the top, and only a select few make it with you all the way. But it doesn't matter when you get there. You reach the summit, and you see the beautiful sunset on the horizon. You did the work yourself, and you get to enjoy the view. A view that isn't cluttered by the people who weren't able to or decided not to show up fully. In fact, you have to turn around to see those halfasses at all.

OK, that's not really fair...they aren't halfasses. That was just me wanting to be super supportive for you because you're awesome and deserve for everyone in your life to show up fully. But we'll take this moment to be true and honest; just because someone decides halfway up the climb that it's not THEIR climb to climb, doesn't make them halfasses. It makes them human and on their own path. And when you focus on you and your journey to the top, it's not about deciding who is worth the invite or who is worth sharing the view. It's about allowing the space for every human in your life to occupy their own path. And being OK with the decision to not join yours. Again, not a decision for you to make; they will decide that on their own.

Honoring Yourself

Notice the impact that living in integrity has on everyone around you. You never need to convince anyone to change or attempt to change their path for them. Remember to respect every human's individuality. There are several things I see People Pleasers do as they recover. Here are behaviors to look out for:

- Pitying people for not being on your level is not the type of empowerment you should aspire to. To the Pleaser sitting on their throne believing they know what's best for everyone else, what if the reality is this … Maybe you don't know shit, and the people you thought didn't know shit could actually teach you some shit you didn't know you needed to know … Oh shit!
- Respect each human's individual journey and the unique quality that it is, especially if it looks nothing like your own. Don't fall into the new-age wokeness ego of, "Oh well, I don't need to bring anyone

with me because they're just not on my level."
You may not agree with their path, but maybe they
are struggling with their own addictions. Their path
is uniquely beautiful to them and is meant to get
them wherever they're destined to go. That doesn't
mean your path is better, and it doesn't mean they
don't have the same incredible gifts to offer this
world that you do.

- Be careful with over-processing, and avoid coaching others. When a Pleaser awakens, it can be a
  very exciting time. They want to coach everyone
  and dive into every little feeling. Unfortunately,
  over-processing can become a burden and take
  away the joy of the work you've done thus far.
  Don't berate yourself if you find yourself in this
  space. Instead, just recognize it. Any time you slip
  up, recognize the growth. Give yourself a high five
  that you caught it and move on. And above all,
  practice humility when your loved ones call you on
  your shit! "Stop trying to fix me!" or "Stop coaching
  me!" ... these can be confronting, but you need to
  take a step back. Respect the human and your own
  recovery with a genuine, "Ew, you're absolutely
  right! I'm sorry. It was not my intention to make
  you feel belittled or unseen! How would you like
  me to support you in this?"

You Can't *Settle* for HAPPY

In building these new relationships, it's important to know you can't continue to hold the anxiety that something better is out there.

Stop me if you've heard this one before: The worst decision is indecision. Aha moment or eyeroll, it's undeniably true. So instead, connect with the feeling of unease, and make a decision based on that clarity rather than existing in indecision and anxiety loops.

My friend is in this new, sweet, blossoming relationship, and her boyfriend had to go out of the country for Mission work. They opted to try to make it work long distance, but she was concerned when she didn't miss him more. Over a cocktail she told me, "I'm worried that by being with this person with whom I'm not experiencing the depths of passion I think I could (or should) be, I'm closing off the doors for other opportunities to come to me energetically." She feared missing out on something mind-blowing because she was merely "enjoying" her relationship rather than feeling utterly consumed by it.

I shared the story of my ex-husband. I never knew I was unhappy with him until I felt happy with someone else. But I wasn't worrying whether someone better existed. That didn't stop it from showing up in my life. Your anxiety and overthinking aren't what invite the best life to you. Your self love is. Your anxiety IS a guaranteed way to fuck up the good stuff you might have going now. And anxious cloudy energy is a damn sure way to push away something twice as amazing if it were trying to find you. Allowing yourself to exist within your current happiness doesn't form a wall of resistance for your destiny. Destiny ain't dumb. She WILL happen, whether you're ready for her or not. Find and name your unhappy before you decide it must be a sense of buyer's remorse. Pitbulls, especially, will lose their attraction to a purchase simply based on the nagging thought that there was another better or cheaper version of it out there somewhere.

As long as you're happy, there's no such thing as settling. Worrying something better is out there is NOT the same thing as being unhappy. When you have this fear, sit with yourself, get into the present, and ask, "Am I actually unhappy about something?" If there is something there, you can explore it and make decisions about it. Being unsure is a natural part of existing with a lack of identity and the inability to trust yourself. The more you show up to your own life, the stronger and more beautifully your identity will form. And the stronger your identity, the stronger your trust in yourself.

The Wedding Funeral

Melissa, a graduate of my original People Pleasers Autonomous™ BETA program, tells the story of how she confronted her People Pleasing addiction by planning a southern wedding in two days.

She had already been rushing to plan her wedding because there was nothing she wanted more than to be wed in her mother's presence, but her mother had been confined to hospice, and the prognosis was already short.

While planning the wedding, Melissa received the news she couldn't "happy thought" her way out of. The prognosis was suddenly shortened, and her mother had mere days left on this earth. So despite the looks from her relatives and the "Wow, you're really going to make this about you?" eyerolls from her siblings, Melissa took a deep breath and said, "Fuck it, we're doing this, and we're doing it now. If my mom only has two days to live, then that's how fast I'm going to plan a wedding. I want to be there, hold her hand, hug her one last time, and let her know her baby girl is absolutely taken care of and in good hands." Her mother passed before the wedding came.

This isn't a sad story. This is the story of how Melissa confronted her need for approval. Normally she would have played caregiver to everyone around her during this tragedy. Instead, she held her own needs in her heart. She followed the

YES within and moved toward what made her soul happy.

And guess what? She survived. She wasn't shunned by her loved ones. She wasn't discarded as unworthy of their love simply because they didn't understand her and she went against their ideals.

In the face of one of the strongest triggers a People Pleaser can be confronted with, Melissa took it by the balls and said, "Not today, PPA, I've got an inner child to listen to!"

She and her fiancé were married in a beautiful ceremony just a few days later.

Asking Without Guilt

When you know what you want, you can ask without guilt. Whether it's food, sex, or respect from other humans, trust that if you speak up for yourself, they will do the same.

It's a process. Your family, significant other(s), and friends won't know how to interact with you. Everything will change. You will argue differently. You will celebrate differently. You will respond to triggers differently.

The key is to let them know what you're doing. Surrender and take the burden off the both of you. Tell them, "No matter what, I surrender completely to your honesty." That's your way of telling them that you will believe them the first time they tell you something. There will be no more obsessing after the fact or asking repeatedly, "Are you sure?"

Tell them you trust them, you trust that they are being true to themselves, and you ask that they do the same for you.

This conversation can significantly help a relationship in struggle. When you start to spiral, your partner can pull you back to the present and remind you, "Hey, you said you were going to trust me." Your neuro-system can sigh in relief and stop spinning.

If what you want still seems like a scary blank canvas, you'll love the Nightmare List practice later in this chapter!

A Purely Authentic Life is Possible

Remove the need to overexplain or convince others of your motivation, intentions, or existence. The moment you find yourself doing any of these, pause and ask yourself, "Who am I trying to convince? Why do I feel like they need convincing? Am I convinced?"

If you are convinced, stop talking. You are all that matters in this situation, so if you're convinced about whatever you find yourself overexplaining to someone, you can literally just *stop*. If you aren't convinced, then you can excuse yourself and dig deeper into how you truly feel about the situation at hand. Something as simple as, "You know, that's a good question, let me check in deeper with myself and we can come back to that when I'm fully resourced," can be such an elegant, self-respecting, take-no-shit, I-said-what-I-fuckin-said response to anyone contradicting your share. Whether it's simply a point of view you've yet to consider, or someone is legitimately gaslighting you, or even if you're gaslighting yourself!

Having confidence in the thing you're overexplaining is the entire goal. It makes everyone else's opinions null and void. If you lack that confidence, it could be because historically, this person or crowd has made you second-guess yourself. Or the lack of confidence may be the result of you ignoring an intuitive pull that something isn't right about the thing you are overexplaining.

If you aren't convinced, ask yourself, "Do I trust this person I'm overexplaining to?" If the answer is no, then why the fuck are you overexplaining? You have my permission to calmly say, with a beautiful smile on your face, "Ha! Wow. I'm confident in this, and if you have a different view about it, that's really none of my business. I'm done overexplaining." If the answer is yes, you do trust this person, then you're overexplaining to convince yourself, and that's something to take home and mull over very seriously.

Shitters & Falsies

Finding confidence in your truly authentic voice is possible, and it has nothing to do with stripping down to your core essence or loading up your esthetic with flare. It's about doing what feels good. Right then and there. In the moment.

I once spent an hour on my makeup (I even popped on some false eyelashes), and at the end a friend FaceTimed me.

"Your life is so glamorous! It's 2:00 p.m. and you're getting all dolled up in whatever city your beautiful giant RV is in today. I don't think I could pull off that kind of spontaneous life with that much class."

What she didn't know was there is a secret to authenticity. It's not about being who you are now. It's about being who you didn't even know you could be. But YOU have to believe the shit you're selling. Believe it with your eyes, your style, your voice, your laugh ... hell you can even change the way you sneeze! But YOU have to buy it too. Once you do, you've achieved authenticity. And it's not because you have a new group of friends who don't know the old you. It's not because you became good at pretending to be more than you thought you were.

It's about knowing that you are the one who puts limits on yourself.

It's not society that says you can't wear that shade of lipstick, it's actually you.

It's not your lover who says you shouldn't expose your midriff or wear that low-cut blouse, it's you.

It's not your mother who says you shouldn't wear that frumpy smock dress or overalls. It's you!

Whatever your inner child is begging you to do, put on, or wear ... DO IT.

And once you do, don't listen to a single person who questions you, because the moment you do, you're looking your soul in the face and telling her she's wrong. That's the real A word y'all. The AUDACITY to have your soul's BACK in the face of your crippling need for approval.

Despite that epic rant, my friend didn't believe a word I said.

So I sent her a video of me posing fiercely, fully dressed, hair dopely coiffed, contour that could cut a bitch, and falsies flappin ... squatting over an ill-fitting sewer entry, guiding a giant poop-hose into a janky hole, pulling the evacuation lever, and noisily flushing out my Entegra Aspire's 41-gallon black tank.

Her response?

"Oh my god! You've never looked more like a model!" She saw the Authentic me. Not because I was faking anything. But because I did as my inner child asked and glammed it the fuck up.

Knowing I had NOWHERE to be and NOTH-ING to do that night except empty the black tank.

It took her almost 15 minutes to see the rest of the scenery past my authenticity.

"Wait ... OMG are you vogueing over the shitter???"

To which I said simply, "Shitters and falsies baby ... Shitters and falsies. Do you believe me now?"

Design the Support You Require

You want to surround yourself with the people who matter, so now is the time to design the support you require.

This concept is a bit of a departure from gratitude journaling or manifesting and knowing what you're worthy of and drawing it to you. Because the flip side of knowing what you want is actually knowing what you DON'T want.

A lot of the work we've done is about respecting the human, which can make us a little too forgiving. For a Pleaser who is rebuilding their identity, really the only resounding answer for what you want is, "I'm not going to put up with abuse anymore." But there's still more to it.

In this section, you're going to create a vision board of your nightmare avatar. Knowing what you WANT to attract is much easier when you know what you don't want and what you won't put up with!

Take out a sheet of paper and write down a list of deal-breakers. Write all the nightmare versions of your least ideal friends or partner(s). Perhaps it's someone who is chronically late or someone who doesn't respond to texts in a timely manner. Someone who is offensive or rude to your friends. Someone who looks down on your romantic partner(s).

This may sound easy, but it can be a little heavy and bring up past abuses. The things you write down will most likely be attributes and scenarios you've experienced in one way or another.

Take as much time as you need. Know that you can repeat this practice anytime you wish, so there's no need to get antsy if you hit a block and can only think of one thing. Clearly that one thing is what wants to be seen!

It's time to put your foot down.

Once you have your list, move to a clean sheet of paper, and write down the opposite of each shitty item. Create the beautiful versions of the humans you want to attract into your life.

This will help you really narrow down what you want, rather than starting from scratch with a fluffy list of bullshit. You will zero in on the exact type of people you are looking to attract.

Now take your Nightmare List and light that shit on fire. Literally. And take your desired support list and put it somewhere special. You can use this practice for any element in which you're feeling discontent with its current quality. Your dream home, your dream work partner, your dream relationship with your parents. Anything. This is YOUR dream now. And you can't bring it to fruition by hiding from your nightmares.

Truly Respect the Body and Mind

You're now attracting the people you want in your life, but there's still some work to do. It's time to repair the language spoken between your mind and body and flex your physical intuition.

This is my Bless and Release practice. Most People Pleasers loathe this practice in the beginning, but it's necessary for your recovery and healing.

Your fears have led you to believe some fucked up things about yourself. Don't you want to look in the mirror and see a god/goddess/non-binary ethereal being? Not just your physical appearance, but an alignment between what you THINK you're going to see and what you ACTUALLY see?

This practice will begin to hone your gift of recognizing physical manifestations of what's going on in your life. But first it will allow you to release the fears and pain you are holding in your body.

The first step is to get naked.

Fully nakey.

Whether it's at the beginning of the day, end of the day, or whenever … strip down. Even your makeup!

Now, get very close to your mirror, just a few inches away. For sixty seconds, look into your own eyes.

It sounds simple, mundane, and time consuming … but we NEVER look into our own eyes.

A lot is going to happen, but your subconscious will take care of it all and begin to repair the connection between your mind and your vision. No need to process or diagnose anything here. Just be with your eyes.

After 60 seconds, step back so you can see your entire body. (If you need to buy a full body mirror, go do it!) Look at your reflection. Take inventory. Look at the shape, the scars, the stretch marks, the curves, the bones, the fat. Turn around. Turn to the side. Look at everything.

The first time you do this, it can take five minutes or more! It may not feel sexy, but the goal is to just get to know your body again. Many don't look in the mirror until they have on their most flattering jeans. That's a fabrication.

As you take inventory, I want you to take notes. Every single time you have a negative thought about your body, write it down. Do NOT dismiss these thoughts. Every single negative thought needs to rise to the surface and be documented. They need to be heard. These thoughts are still you! Don't stifle them or change them or pretty them up.

Once you have your list, square up with the mirror, look your body up and down, and speak into the areas that elicited the most negative responses. Tell yourself, "Thank you." Pour love into those areas by taking full responsibility that they are there. Speak this healing phrase to your beautiful body:

"When I abused you, you loved me. When I neglected you, you took care of me. When I commanded you, you obeyed. When I abandoned you, you kept me alive."

Everything your body is, is because it was following YOUR orders.

Hug those areas. Say thank you.

And then, take the list with you. Revisit it at some point later in the day, and use the below conversions to change those negative thoughts to not just positive ones, but realistic ones!

Stop Talkin' That 'ish!

Here is a positive self-talk conversion chart with the goal of going from the left side to the right!

"I've let myself GO" | "I stopped putting myself FIRST"

"This is too HARD" | "This is what getting STRONGER feels like!"

"I HATE my..." | "I no longer need this piece of ARMOR I've created"

"I'll NEVER..." | "I haven't YET..."

"The PROBLEM is..." | "My newest exciting OBSTACLE is..."

"What's WRONG with me?" | "Where have I fallen out of INTEGRITY with myself?"

"My GOAL weight/size is..." | "My HAPPIEST self IS my HEALTHIEST self!"

"I WOULD! But my <insert person(s)> won't..." | "I WILL! Because the opinions, actions, or INactions of others have nothing to do with ME!"

"I'm NOT <blank> enough" | "I am an act of Self Love and Recovery in motion! I am fucking PERFECT!"

Escapism Vs. Nurturing Your Inner Child

There is a difference between escapism and nurturing your inner child. If you still emotionally abuse your inner child, you need to cut that shit out! It's not a weakness to acknowledge your inner child's needs, and it's not a strength to ignore them.

If there's something childlike you want to do, do it. If you want to buy a coloring book, buy a fucking coloring book. Don't let anyone say shit about it! If you want to sit and color, you need to listen to that part of yourself. Your nervous system is begging for a known safety cue. Give it what it wants. It's on your side.

As a society, we've gotten so good at keeping our inner child silent and telling it to go sit in the corner and be quiet. Don't. Be a child and go through the day without worry. Mending your relationship with your inner child is a massive step.

Every trigger response, physiological response, and emotional response is linked to the traumas that occurred in your developmental stages in life.

INTERNAL GASLIGHTING: Emotional Trauma has no minimum requirement. Trauma describes anything that occurs with either sudden or consistent impact that creates a neuro-system response moving forward.

These emotional trauma response patterns that were created can be healed and new patterns adopted to support your nervous system and create an emotionally safe environment.

You can begin this process simply by asking in any given anxiety bubble, "What is little me asking for right now??" and writing that little you a letter, acknowledging them and their pain, and promising to have their back moving forward.

Dear 16-Year-Old Ahdri

I'm taking a break from revising my manuscript to tell you something important.

I'm sorry.

I'm sorry we dove into the humans around us for validation because we didn't know what trauma was or how to heal it.

I'm sorry I didn't listen when you cried.

I'm sorry I didn't build you up from the inside.

I'm sorry I bound your hands and pushed you through the motions.

I'm sorry I sold your heart and your body to the highest bidder.

But I'm so grateful....

For the lessons these last 19 years have taught us.

The space we were allowed to occupy in the gracious hearts of the men who held us.

And the clarity this body of ours is now existing in.

And for these reasons I will no longer apologize to you about these transgressions.

I will no longer put the burden of your forgiveness on your shoulders.

I will instead hold your hand.

I will instead show you—through consistency—
that you're protected, that we are safe.
In solidarity.
Because now more than ever, I can hear you, and if
you'll trust me, I can hold you.
I love you.

Managing Your Energy

Your energy is affected by other people's energies.
No really, much like co-regulation between our nervous
systems!

And even if you're already on the same page with me
on this, you might not be fully aware of the full weight of
the situation and what it's costing you.

We have energy outpouring constantly, in little tethers to memories, people, conversations we're afraid of
having, conversations we've had, etc. They are like spi-
derwebs stretching from you, even while you're sleeping.
And energy can only flow outward through them. So it's
important to consistently sever their connections to others so your energy can remain grounded in your own
body. You know the old saying, "You can't pour from an
empty cup"? Well this is quite literally the manifestation
of that reality!

There's a practice you can do, even in public, to get
rid of all these thoughts that spiral. You are going to

"clear the cache" with Cord Cutting. This tool is taught under different names by so many different energy healers around the globe; my favorite technique comes from Sheevaun Moren.

Visualize these beautiful glistening cords stretching from your abdomen, your throat, your crown, your back, your groin, and then some. They extend out into the world—to people in the same room, to situations that haunt you from your past, and to impossible distances where people you don't even realize are linked to your subconscious. Your energy will pour into anyone and anything willing to take it while it's tethered, and it's time to cut them off.

Gather the threads stretching away from you and cut them. You can do it in a huge gesture if that feels gratifying. Begin with your arms outstretched, your palms facing each other, one over your head and just in front of you, and one at its natural groin level. Slowly bring them together and visualize the threads extending out from you gathering in between your hands. As your palms touch at diaphragm level, hold all of the cords in your left hand and pull them taut from your torso. Using the side of your right hand, karate chop that shit with three strong slices between your body and your left hand. You now hold the severed cords in your left hand and can toss that shit away (NOT AT OTHER PEOPLE ... that's rude as hell). Just imagine a 50-foot hole in the ground, toss them in, and kiss those bitches goodbye! Or, if you're in public and feeling self-conscious, just pretend to pull some cobwebs off your body or brush the "cat hair" off your clothing.

The key is to be cognizant of why you're doing it. Know that you're cutting the cords and think these words to yourself: "I'm gathering all the cords ... I'm cutting all the cords."

This process instantly diffuses and discharges the anxious energy drawing you away from being present. I personally do this all throughout the day (especially as someone in the caregiving/emotional wellness industry!) and before I go to bed, because you're going to get some shitty sleep if your energy is constantly sliding down those tethers.

It's the equivalent of clearing your computer cache or shutting down all the open apps on your phone for the day.

Cutting the cords allows you to choose where your energy goes, rather than allowing people and events to suck the energy from you.

Don't believe in all the hoojaboo? Try it anyway, especially in intense situations in which you would otherwise find yourself co-regulating with another human.

Having an intense conversation with your mother and your tongue hurts from biting it? Cut your cords! Keep your energy for you and see how much easier it is to communicate with her in this relaxed, replenishing space of energy efficiency.

Trusting Your Passion Pulls

Passion pulls are what I call our internal navigation or intuitive pulls. Whether you believe in fate or the randomness of free will, your passions are shaped by your experiences and choices up to this very point in time. You are energetically drawn to a matching positive energy that will lead to the next big thing in your life. Whether you can hear or feel that pull is another story.

Your energy is naturally going to pull you, because your energy is designed for the next form of growth or enlightenment. But we've gotten really good at silencing our pulls and becoming completely numb to them.

Internal navigation also helps secure the idea of our own identity. You might find yourself in an argument over what to have for dinner, or have zero input whatsoever, because you don't even know what you like anymore. It can become uncomfortable to sit in silence and figure out what's best for you.

But getting in touch with your true identity isn't as heady as it sometimes seems.

When something gets you excited in a scary way, that's a passion pull. It doesn't have to be huge—like entertaining the idea for a new job or skydiving—but now is the time to get into the practice of feeling them and following them. Don't question them. Don't decide if they are worth your time or side eye them like a weary investment. Don't wonder if it's childish to indulge them. Just do it!

Go to the beach today. Listen to music loudly while doing the dishes. Listen to the tiny things that your normal, over-bearing voice would immediately shut down.

As you begin to do these things more and answer your passion pulls, you will see how good it feels to actually answer them. The bigger passion pulls will get louder, and then you will really start to feel the difference between over-thinking, feeling nervous, and the excitement of a passion pull.

As you give your attention to these pulls and begin to follow them, you will find yourself living more and more in true alignment, unencumbered by self-doubt.

You Won't Fail ...

"Failure" is hate speech for the experiences necessary for your next big thing. If something fails, that wasn't the point. Perhaps you opt to quit your job to open a bakery. If the bakery is a failure, perhaps you met someone during that time and that's the next step on your path.

Having intuition and passion pulls means that you don't have to figure out why they are there! You don't ever have to figure out the reason.

Worrying about failure is another way to second-guess yourself. Never use failure as a reason to silence your pulls. Worrying whether a passion pull will be fruitful is like worrying if you're going to breathe today. Thank God your lungs don't actually need your overthinking input to do their job ... and neither do your passion pulls.

... And You Don't Need Permission

You don't second guess Google Maps! People Pleasers seek affirmation and validation, as they are very deeply linked into our value system and how we see ourselves. Thus, it's hard not to second-guess our passion pulls and ask others what they think.

But it doesn't matter what they think. You don't need anyone's permission to move in ANY direction! Unless, you know, it's your significant other and you're feeling a pull to move across the country. That probably warrants a discussion!

But Pleasers have this tendency to self-sabotage and go straight to the person they know will disagree. You do it because you feel that you don't deserve it. The sensible adult in you wants someone to quickly talk you out of moving forward.

Don't second-guess, though! Your intuition already said, "This is what we should be doing." When you go asking others for their opinions, you're actually seeking permission outside of your soul. Meanwhile your intuition is thinking, "Seriously? I already gave you the clear-cut answer. Who are you asking? What is your problem?" Indulging in sabotaging your pulls is what deafened you to them. So when you can hear one, remember what a gift that is and don't you dare look that gift horse in the mouth.

Fine-Tuning Your Pulls

Most People Pleasers get excited about a passion pull and slink into it, especially their first big one. They kind of test the waters, dip their toe, and think, "This is scary but I'm going to do it!"

Then, out of fear, they marry that idea. They get wrapped up in it, overcommit, and then become afraid of change. They're obsessed with the idea of failure and end up wrecking it. They don't get what they needed, they become unhappy, and then they are on a different trajectory than was ever intended.

So, the key is to play the field a little. Don't marry a passion pull. Nobody gets the house in the divorce! Just date … wildly and with reckless abandon. Jump from one passion pull to another. Don't judge yourself. Don't tell yourself, "No, I decided to do this and thus I have no choice and have to follow through." Follow the next pull, because that's the path you're being pulled on. Each pull is a link on a bourgeoisie chain! And you don't want to get stuck following one link around and around and around.

Know that it's okay to let go. You can release the previous pull. It wasn't wrong. As I said before, it wasn't a failure. It was part of your journey.

Your pulls, your intuitions, your muses … they all have a mind of their own. And they get offended! They don't need your anxiety, commitment, and weirdness. They need your action. And if you don't take them seriously, they'll move on to someone else in the blink of an eye.

Exist on a Higher Love-Fueled Frequency

You WILL fall. You WILL mess up. You WILL act out of character. You WILL speak out of turn. You WILL surprise yourself! But if you are consistent in acting out of passion and love, redemption for those shit moments is inevitable and does not require your flagellation … ever.

Existing on such a frequency is reciprocal. The energy and respect you protect and feed into yourself create not only the energy and respect you'll receive in return but the energy and respect you can pour into others. Your loved ones don't deserve your tired, desperate tidbits. They deserve the real, nourished you. And only the pieces you wish to share with them. (Your loved ones being deserving of the most authentic you should never obligate you to deliver it.) You don't have to leave the faucet on! And it's an exquisite thing to retain and enjoy yourself … yourself!

Take this moment with me now to celebrate YOU! Celebrate the devotion, the tenacity, the fire you've nurtured through this entire experience. From the strength that made you open this book to the recovered autonomy that helped you finish it. This life IS you. And you are all that matters.

Whether you're feeling amped the fuck up or scared shitless, YOU ARE PERFECT FOR IT. And if you choose to take the challenge of your recovery to the limit with every gorgeous bone, breath, and tear in your body, this world won't even know what's about to hit it. The tools, the resources, and the power you now embody will. Change lives! Starting with the most important of them all, yours. And I can't thank you enough for that. But I will absolutely try ...

Thank you for reclaiming your Autonomy with me.

Thank you for reclaiming the beautiful blank canvas of your identity with me.

Thank you for becoming a fierce fucking light in the darkness of our shared Addiction with me.

Thank you for changing the world simply by loving yourself from this day forward.

Thank you.

Thank you.

Thank you.

I fucking love you.

Acknowledgments

Katrina: For being the big sister of all big sisters. For protecting me. For supporting me. For adoring me. For letting me watch you from behind the legs of grown-ups as you took on the world with arms flung open. For running with me through this life like reckless toddlers amidst sharp corners. For being unshakably YOU.

Juliette: For giving me the opportunity to be anything and everything I could ever dream, with your life, your love, and your unwavering support and excitement. For the times you were right, and for accepting my need to heal from the times you were wrong.

Hans: For making me. For breaking me. The worst of you is gone, I am grateful for that. But I miss you every day. Thank you for gifting me the best parts of you to carry on.

Sean: For being my ride or die in such youthful pivotal years, for knowing and loving my father, for letting me know and love yours. For trusting me with our friendship no matter the forms it has taken in the many years since those sweet 11-year-olds were first introduced in that shithole Conyers, GA, IHOP.

Kelley: For seeing me clearly. Always and forever. For ugly crying for me every time I ever accomplished anything. For never taking a moment's pause before celebrating each and every evolution of myself. For being the dopest drinking buddy cheerleader I could ever hope to have in my corner.

Lamonique: For being such a fucking Queen and non-people-pleasing force in my life that even without being mentioned IN the book, I can't go a single day without speaking your name.

Jess: For the exquisite honor of being one of your Lioness Women.

Amanda: For seeing me so intentionally from the first moment. For making the soul-deep commitment to be too much with me in this life. For continuing to grow with me every damn day, no matter the discomfort. For sharing your gifts, journey, and life with me in so many ways. Let's be red together forever, okay?

Matthew: For playing roles in each other's lives so far removed from what we initially thought. For triggering me, allowing me to trigger you. For your gifts, your lessons, and your love.

My Incredible Clients: For letting me in. For sharing your dedication to yourselves with me. Without you, a huge part of me simply would not exist.

Bill: For the subtle traumas. For filling the house with tones from your golden trumpet. For the Wurlitzer. For what would become my inner child's sanctuary. For music.

My Beloved Music Fans: For your attention, your praise, your adoration, your humor, and your love. We aren't done yet.

Jayne: For creating space in your gorgeous world for my love. And for this dope-ass cover.

Jordan: For cracking me open. For being so impossibly you I question reality every morning. Do you really exist? Do I really get to be this happy? Oh ... and for helping me finish this manuscript with the sexiest bribe ever uttered from a woman's lips.

My Ex-Husband: For being the recipient of my hardest, most destructive, self-indulgent, caretaking love.

Derren: For doing 11 years of this life with me. In all the good ways and the bad. For loving me as deeply as you possibly could. For moving through so much space and time with me. For learning with me and from me. For walking through every transition in my life holding my hand fiercely and shouldering half the fear. I don't regret the regrets, and neither should you.

F: For being one of the truest reflections of Ahdri before shit went sideways. For trusting me so deeply with your friendship, life and love.

Discover what type of
People Pleasing Addict
you are with this free quiz!

Go to
www.ahdri.com/freequiz

Readers' Continued Journey

Recovery, of any kind, never has to be alone.

Visit Ahdri.com to find out how you can become part of the Whimsical Rebellion and continue your journey with us at Patreon with access to community-only q&a's, bonus content, support, and togetherness.

Explore even more opportunities for connection at live events, concerts, book readings, and more.

You love BIG, let us love you BIG right back!

Connect with Ahdri

◎ @therealahdri

f Facebook.com/therealahdri

Stay tuned for Ahdri's next groundbreaking project, a riveting memoir with a fully integrated album woven into the reader experience. (Think: reading along, "Oh look a QR code," headphones, Ahdri's voice and piano soaring sonically through unfuckingbelievable pain and growth, accidental ugly crying, rinse, repeat.)

Through shadow and light, journey with Ahdri through a fusion of unguarded narrative storytelling and viscerally relevant songwriting. You won't want to miss this rare art-driven exposition; a sonic and literary chronicle of one multifaceted artist and the inevitable evolution that dots the timeline of a seeker, a finder. A Whimsical Rebel indeed.